Release and Deployment

An ITSM narrative account

Release and Deployment

An ITSM narrative account

DANIEL McLEAN

it gp™

IT Governance Publishing

IT Governance Publishing
IT Governance Limited
Unit 3, Clive Court
Bartholomew's Walk
Cambridgeshire Business Park
Ely
Cambridgeshire
CB7 4EA
United Kingdom

www.itgovernance.co.uk

First published in the United Kingdom in 2015
by IT Governance Publishing

ISBN 978-1-84928-777-7

PREFACE

During a consulting engagement, I was interviewing a high performing and very successful EVP of sales for a multi-billion dollar company. We discussed IT, its role in leveraging business capabilities, and its historical performance in providing that leverage at his company.

I told him I was trying to identify what IT could do to provide the greatest amount of leverage for the business. If it were up to him, what would he have IT concentrate on above all else? What would he like IT to have as its number one priority?

I expected a laundry list of technology tools to aid in managing his sales force, prospects and customers. I was a little surprised at his instant response, "Don't break anything that's working." There is tremendous insight and truth in what he said.

There are some best practice processes that are foundational and need to be implemented first. There are others that can be enabled more slowly.

Imagine you're the head of a company whose IT organization can't effectively restore service after incidents. When a business service fails, IT might or might not be able to get it working, or even know what to do to make it work again.

If you can't depend on IT to restore service, then you would either want to change the people in your IT organization, or come up with another way to provide that business leverage.

Preface

Just as an effective incident management process is required in any IT organization, so is an equally effective release and deployment process. They are part of the group of best practice processes needed from the start.

Much of the work involved in enabling release and deployment processes involves changing how people work. The words, "People – Process – Tools," are in that order for a reason. If People don't embrace the activity, then the Process and Tools won't matter. Changing people's behavior is one of the hardest things we do in business and something IT people find most difficult.

High performing IT organizations learn how to change people's behavior as easily as they change technologies. Changing behavior is one of the most difficult things you will ever do in business. IT is often at a disadvantage because IT organizations are not known for their strong people skills but that doesn't mean they can't learn.

This is one in a series of books designed to help you understand how others implemented new processes and made the necessary changes to people's behavior.

These fictionalized narratives are based on the actual experience of people just like you ... dealing with the same types of people and issues you face every day.

Look at what worked ... see what failed ... understand the traps to avoid. Learn from the characters' successes and avoid their mistakes.

ABOUT THE AUTHOR

Mr McLean is a consultant who has designed, implemented and operated processes supporting ITSM for over 12 years. He has worked in IT for over 20 years.

He has been involved in the development of global best practice standards and courseware customized to company-specific operational practices and needs. He has worked in the US and the Middle East.

Mr McLean is the author of *The ITSM Iron Triangle: Incidents, Changes and Problems, No One of Us Is As Strong As All of Us: Services, Catalogs and Portfolios, Integrated Measurement – KPIs and Metrics for ITSM* and *Availability and Capacity Management in the Cloud*.

These narratives are designed as both standalone works and components of a larger integrated story arc covering the ITSM world and its challenges.

Mr McLean's consultancy focuses on fusing best practices from multiple ITSM standards into practical operational processes, optimized for each organization's particular environment and needs. He provides this support at the design, implementation and daily operation levels.

Among other honors, Mr McLean holds multiple ITSM related best practice and ISO/IEC certificates.

Mr McLean holds both Bachelor's and Master's degrees from Cornell University.

Mr McLean resides in Chicago, Illinois, US.

ACKNOWLEDGEMENTS

I wish to thank the following people, without whom none of this would have been possible.

My clients, users and customers, for allowing me to learn and improve by serving them.

My managers and leaders, for trusting me with opportunities that make me grow.

My peers, for challenging my habits and making me continually assess and improve my deliverables.

My manuscript reviewers: Chris Evans, ITSM specialist, Dave Jones, Pink Elephant and ir. H.L. (Maarten) Souw RE, Enterprise Risk and QA Manager, UVW, for their insightful and constructive guidance.

My editors, proofreaders, publishing, marketing and other associates at IT Governance Publishing, for their incredible patience and tireless support, especially Vicki Utting.

My teachers and mentors, for their tolerance of my ignorance, persistence in their instruction, and patience with my endless questions.

My employees, students and mentees, for allowing me to grow by helping them learn.

My family, for tolerating my single-minded focus.

And my wife, Patricia, for being my rock and constant companion.

CONTENTS

INTRODUCTION

No IT organization can survive for long without an effective release and deployment process.

Without it, IT will either be supplanted by a third party organization at the demands of the business, or the entire company will collapse. An IT organization without an effective release and deployment process is like an IT organization without incident or change management.

Like a public utility, release and deployment is highly visible only when its failures disrupt the business. When done correctly, very little activity should be visible to the business.

Release and deployment processes exist to plan, build, test, schedule, and control the deployment into production of releases that will increase the capabilities of the business without damaging the integrity of the current services.

Release and deployment touches virtually all of the ITSM processes. Each one of those connections presents a risk of failure points that need to be managed. There are so many ways release and deployment can vividly fail that it is a testament to the skill and commitment of those involved when it quietly succeeds without notice by others.

But not every release deployed into production goes smoothly. When something does go wrong, a trickle of calls and alerts can quickly become an avalanche. The service desk is soon overwhelmed with calls from users. The pagers and phones of the development and support teams light up at all hours of the day. Senior business leaders are on the phone to the leadership of IT yelling about lost revenue and threatening replacement by third parties.

Within IT, the finger of blame always points to the owners of the impacting process – Release. This is unfair and displays the confusion that often exists in IT about the exact nature of deploying releases, who is involved, and the ways in which things can go wrong.

At its simplest level, release is a noun, describing a number of changes which are built and tested to be deployed together. Deployment is a verb describing the enablement of a release in the live production environment.

The actual introduction of the release into live production is just the tip of a process that interacts with a number of other organizations, such as application development, quality assurance, infrastructure, business relationship management, change, finance and others. The challenge is that these organizations are not normally part of the release manager's team, except on a loan and as available basis. Regardless, the release and deployment manager remains accountable for the result.

To succeed in that role, release and deployment managers need to successfully navigate the web of relationships between those groups and, more importantly, the people in those organizations. Success is highly dependent on the ability to manage, by influence, those other teams. In this case that means not just managing your relationships with others but also helping them manage their relationships with each other.

This is especially true in the foundational area of business requirements and its critical link with design and development. You often see IT organizations celebrate their activity and achievement, only to find out they have failed to meet the needs of the business. They failed because they were successful at doing the wrong thing. They did it right but it was not what the business needed.

The minimum essential steps that need to be taken are to empower a role gathering the business requirements, ensure it is tightly coordinated with design and development in a way that is responsive to the dynamic business environment, and charge the release manager with building connections between the functional knowledge towers. That level of agile engagement is difficult. Even with the right person in place, it takes practice and time to become proficient.

The next time someone raises questions about resourcing release and deployment, or delaying its enablement, tell them that these are not essential questions.

Remind them that the real question is, "Do you and your IT organization want to survive"?

All actions, places, organizations, people and events described, while based on real experiences, are fictitious. Any resemblance to real people, living or dead, is entirely coincidental. Any resemblance to actual places, organizations or events is entirely coincidental.

CHAPTER 1: WINNING THE JOB

Megan rubbed her fingertips against each other, giving the impression she was either praying for guidance or contemplating her prey. She took a slow, very deliberate breath and paused. As the silence filled the room, her smile made it clear she was looking for a victim, not guidance. And it was my bad luck to be the quarry sitting across the desk from her.

I was tired of job hunting. It had been almost four months since Jessica, my boss at the last company, was forced out in some smooth manipulations by a few other directors. Apparently they were jostling for a soon to be announced VP vacancy and she was just the first casualty in what became a sharp-elbowed conflict for supremacy. It was not unusual, just what goes on at that level in most big companies. What I found perplexing was that every time I saw it, the company's senior leadership was well aware of what was happening. They knew it did nothing for the stockholders or the customers, yet stayed out of it and almost encouraged it. Perhaps it was because that is how they all rose to their positions. Or maybe it was their way to determine who had what it takes to work at their level. I'd probably never get the chance to find out.

Once Jessica had been ousted, the other directors created systematic cases to clean out her entire team, regardless of their individual performance. This scorched earth behavior was very standard behavior and they were very efficient at it. About the only thing they didn't do was to salt the earth and conduct some sort of ritual public mutilation.

And of course I was one they pushed out after Jessica.

1: Winning the Job

The job market was still weak in this part of the country, so being forced out of a company was definitely a career threatening situation. I knew there were a lot of candidates for each job in the area. All of them reasonably qualified so it was hard to go wrong. It was just the way employers liked it, because it kept the staff quiet and obsequious. Networking was the only way to find a position and even then you had to stand out from the rest in some unique way. But when almost your entire network is out of work too, it doesn't help you a lot.

Megan leaned across her desk. Her words snapped me back to the interview.

"Tell me, Chris. What makes you more appropriate for this position than the other people I've talked to this week? Why should I take a chance on you"? Then she glanced at her watch and huffed as if she were behind schedule and had three more people waiting outside her office for interviews.

I sat silently for a moment, composing an answer that wouldn't sound like, "Because I'm the best you are going to see and you'd be a fool not to hire me. Release may not be my career aspiration, but I've done this before and am so over-qualified for this role that I can do it standing on my head while holding my breath."

But after all the interviews I'd had over the last couple of months, I knew that would be unwise, unless I was looking to cut the interview very short. I started to speak, but with the exquisite timing of a chess grandmaster, she cut me off.

"Let me put it differently. I just don't understand why you would even consider applying for this job. You'd be bored to tears in a week. I mean, after all, you have an amazing background. You must know so much more about the release and implementation of apps than anyone else here ... even me, and I've been through one of those 'All-Told' fundamental classes for IT services."

I mentally winced at her apparent lack of awareness and understanding. Perhaps this was a test to see if I knew what she was talking about and how, or would, I correct her.

Megan leaned back in her chair, looking oh so contented with her questioning. It was a well-structured inquiry. It was seemingly simple at first glance, but full of complex nuance just below the surface. She had put me in a position where defending my skills would give her a reason to reject me, while down-playing them would also give her a reason to reject me.

I'd researched Megan thoroughly and been lucky enough to discover leadership had parachuted her into this role straight from her work overseeing construction of solutions by the development teams. She'd been incredibly successful building tools, but had little experience in making them useful. I guessed that leadership was testing her with this assignment. This mundane role couldn't be her dream position. She probably viewed it as a way to show that she was the company's next golden child and not some one-hit wonder. My sense was that she was trying to break out of IT and into the business side of the house ... the place where all the advancement, glory and money resided. She seemed experienced enough to know that if she brought me in and I failed as release manager, it would be viewed as a negative on her. And in the hyper-competitive world of director and above, even something as mundane as a bad hire into a key area could be enough to hold you back ... if she were lucky enough to keep her job.

I didn't want her to be threatened by me, but at the same time I wanted her to feel I would have no problem executing the role, and I would present little risk to her career if she hired me. Despite her display of ignorance illustrated through her personal training comment, I didn't need her to know what I knew to succeed. But it was important to her ego that she thought she did. She needed to feel comfortable that I was not a threat to her or her success. And that was her mistake. Managers, who insist they know just as much, if not more than everyone who works for them, are never very effective.

The good news was that people who get parachuted into a situation by leadership almost never have any expectation of having a career in that role. They simply see it as a way to show leadership how good they are at producing results and reinforcing the common mistake weak leadership can make ... namely that a good manager can manage anything, regardless of their background. Once she had reinforced leadership's preconceptions of the world, they would move her to the next crisis and to become their go-to warrior ... at least until she stumbled. Then they would replace her with their next superhero with a cape. To them, she was expendable proof of their superior vision and understanding of the business. After all, they were senior leaders because they possessed those attributes, and anyone whose performance called that into question was clearly substandard and needed to be replaced. Failing to confirm and reinforce that was a sign of a failed superhero, not a gap in leadership assumptions. I'd always found that to be nearly hilarious ... only in a company could the idea flourish that when reality doesn't agree with preconceived assumptions, clearly reality is wrong and will be ignored until it corrects itself and aligns with their assumptions.

1: *Winning the Job*

I struggled to keep wearing my best poker face and reminded myself that people who become senior leadership have some superb insights that we could all benefit from. So I followed the example of many great leaders by answering the question I wanted to answer, not the one Megan had asked.

Shaking my head slightly, I broke eye contact for a moment and looked up at the ceiling. That was an okay kinesthetic. Looking down would have been a disaster. After a moment of silence to encourage her to think she'd thrown me off balance, I looked straight at her, gave a slightly exaggerated sigh and said, "You know, Megan, it is really very sad. Fortunately, the fact that I am here talking to you makes it clear your company gets it. It is tragic so few companies do."

Her mouth parted slightly, as if to speak, but no words came immediately out. A response that jerked the conversation in a different direction by letting me frame my response from a, "can't win" to a, "can't lose" path was not what she had expected. But I was determined to stand out and show her I could play the interview game as well as any.

I pressed the palms of my hands together in front of my face for a moment, before putting my hands palms-down on the desk and leaning a little closer across the desk. Not close enough to violate her personal space, but just enough to make her feel I was very serious ... that I was sharing a deep insight with her ... that I was giving her a special and perhaps even secret message. I lowered the register and volume of my voice. Slowly shaking my head back and forth I said, "The transition of projects into production is where so many companies stumble and so much great development work is wasted."

I sat back a little in my chair. "I'm sure you've seen it before. Uncountable hours of hard work designing, building and testing a brilliant solution, and then when it's time to bring it to life for your customers, it all falls apart at their first touch and no one appears responsible. It falls apart not because anything has changed about the solution. It falls apart because of how the solution is developed, moved into the live environment and integrated with all the other applications."

I slowly shook my head. "It's tragic. That's why I was so excited to see that your senior leadership understood the dynamics and was determined to avoid that happening again by putting someone with your strengths and background in charge of putting the team in place to manage the solution. That's the kind of executive vision and commitment that inspires us all."

I looked up and straight at her. "Don't you agree"? Sometimes a thematic non-answer beats a content rich response.

She nodded, and for the first time in our interview, that smirky smile of power was nowhere to be found on her face.

"Yes," she stumbled, not wanting to sound like she thought senior leaders were making a mistake. Then swallowing hard to regain her composure and show me how insightful she was, she nodded and said, "I've seen it too, of course." After a brief pause, she added a weak face-saving, "At other firms, of course. That's why I agreed to this role, this opportunity to build a team to rescue the company from a faulty process."

I cut her off before she could continue. You had to be careful with thematic answers. Sometimes they induce the other person to ramble around and around your statement, endlessly confirming it. One of the pieces of interview coaching I'd received from my mentors was to always try to turn the interview around, so that they're trying to impress you, not the reverse. "Yes. I could tell you understood the situation. It was very clear from your line of questions in this interview. Your leadership vision made you want to ensure it would be covered for this role by over-hiring the skill set and not relying on someone who only met the minimum qualifications."

By the way she nodded and smiled it was clear she was aligning with me.

She responded with, "That's why they put me in this role … to get the right set of resources and processes in place to ensure we can support the needs of the business."

"Have you begun any efforts to establish a process to make things work better"? I moved the interview away from me to a tactical review of how she was currently addressing the issue, so the focus of our conversation became my reviewing her actions so far, rather than her trying to find a reason to knock me out of the competition.

I already knew the answer because I had done enough research and networked with enough former employees to know that the transition of bright and shiny projects into customer solutions was consistently a train wreck here. And despite the oblique wording of the posting for the position opening, it was clear they didn't have a solution and probably not the will to fix it, even if they knew what the solution should be. That's the role they were really interviewing me for, even though the official position title was, "Project Manager."

That didn't bother me. Almost every company I knew had the same problem. Leadership was always overly impressed with activity, but the grunt work of making it operational and successfully transitioning it into a means of adding value, was too mundane to hold the interest of leadership for extended periods. They just wanted it fixed.

What many missed was that the real value was not in the production of the application itself. There was a lot of incredible work by highly talented people to create something that was often amazing. The teams that made that happen deserved credit and reward for their efforts. But the ultimate value went back to the real purpose of IT – to increase through partnership and technical leverage, the capability of the business to achieve their goals. If we weren't doing that, as far as the company was concerned, we were simply consuming oxygen and reducing the occurrence of rust in the building.

I had a simple question. If they wanted someone to help build a way to successfully integrate projects into the customer's world, why hadn't they been more direct about it. Either they really had no idea of what or how to do it, or there was someone on the grey organization chart who had the job and was failing but hadn't been removed because they had a lot of pull on the grey chart.

Every organization has a formal organization chart as well as a grey chart. The formal chart is the one they show to people and use to give titles. The grey chart is where the real power lies. It's a roadmap to whose voice rings the loudest. The reason so many people struggle with the grey chart is that it is never written down. There are no records and no documents to investigate. The only way you know what it looks like is by paying close attention to the relationship dynamics between people independent of title. If you are lucky a mentor or friend may share what they have learned with you. No one ever seems to know all of the grey chart, only sections of it, and the grey chart is in a constant state of flux. But the more you know, the more you can impact how the company works.

By the time we got to the end of the interview, I was almost confident Megan would recommend hiring me. The way she talked it seemed more like she was selling me on the company than I was selling her on me. It felt really good.

"I was wondering who my direct manager would be in this role? It is a little unusual to get to this point in the interview process and not meet them, or even know who it would be."

She nodded. "We are still structuring the role in the organization. We needed to see the skills and experience of the best candidate before we decided how and where they would fit on the team."

"Oh ... " That sounded like cover for leadership indecision or fighting over reqs.

"But I think that if you are the right person for this opportunity, with your background and experience, moving forward ... rather if we decide to move forward, it makes more sense for you to report directly to me."

I tried to cover my surprise and pleasure at the idea of working directly for a senior leader like Megan, especially one who knew very little and would therefore let me set my own agenda, as long as it advanced her career and position amongst her peers.

By the time I was in the parking lot, I was convinced the job was mine. I made a mental note to make sure everything was in order outside work. I hoped to start this new job quickly because I really needed the money and I wanted to give it my all, especially in the beginning. I knew that a good 90 day halo would stick with you for years if it was strong enough.

Two weeks later, I had a signed sweet job offer and a start date. This was going to be good.

Knowledge that would have helped Chris

- You will often find your immediate boss may not be able to do your job, even if their career depended on it. Remember that is why they hired you. They were smart enough to hire someone who knew a lot more than they did. If you find yourself working for a boss who can do your work as well, or better than you can, you may find yourself working for a micromanager who will focus on how you do your job, as much as what you deliver. Regardless of the type of boss you end up with, your success and survival demands that you determine the level of involvement they need in your work as soon as possible. In other words, knowing how involved your boss wants to be in your job is essential information to your survival.
- Always look at the situation independently from the job description, to see if the two are in sync. Many times the hiring organization will not fully understand what is needed to solve the issue. This will give you a

---

tremendous advantage during your interviewing and hiring negotiations. Being able to take them from what they think they need, to what they may really need, can be a game-winner for you. The risk is that you are talking to someone who is insecure, suffers from hubris, or is otherwise convinced they know more than anyone else.

- When you develop the solution to achieving a goal, there is still a lot more to do. You must also sell your solution to others. Too many ultimately fail, not because they were weak, but because they weren't effectively sold to the right constituencies. Always remember, people are the single biggest contributors to success or failure. Which alternative you get depends on how well you convince people to align with your solution.

CHAPTER 2: WHERE DID MY JOB GO?

It was a bright and fresh Monday morning, my first day on the new job. I'd shown up early, ready to kick butt and take names. It was a clean start and I was excited at the prospect of showing them how a real pro works. To me, this release manager role was just a, "foot in the door" type of position. I didn't expect to be in it for more than a year, so my primary focus was going to be on where I wanted to go next and not on solving their trivial problems.

But it was not to be. At least not yet. I'd been in an HR conference room for what seemed like all morning, filling out an endless series of forms, checking boxes, selecting deductions, making declarations, and generally signing my life away. It was the kind of activity where after an hour or so your mind gets a crusty glaze over it that's harder than a week-old donut. Every time I finished one pile of paper, a very pleasant, perky administrative assistant from HR, named Sophie, handed me a new pile. Around me were a collection of other eager newbs; each filled with hopes and aspirations for this new phase of their career, each demonstrating their eagerness by dutifully working their way through the seemingly endless flow of forms.

Filling in my name and social security number for what seemed like the tenth time, I kept wondering why this wasn't all electronic, with single entry for each data item and set up so we could complete it on a tablet before showing up on our first day. To keep my sanity, I let my mind work on the design of such an onboarding system while slogging through the papers.

Hearing the door open, followed by footsteps, I looked up to see who the new victim was. Megan walked in. She saw me, but didn't acknowledge me in any special way. Instead, she walked directly to Sophie.

After a few whispered words, Sophie said, "I'll be right back. Keep working and I'll help you with any questions when I return," and then stepped out of the room with Megan.

They were gone for only a few moments. Sophie returned by herself, but I could see Megan outside in the hall having a highly animated discussion on her phone.

Sophie walked directly to me, leaned over and whispered in my ear, as if we were in some school exam room, taking our year-end final tests and she didn't want to disrupt the concentration of the other examinees.

"Chris, something very important has come up and it directly affects your new role. Megan has asked to pull you from the onboarding process so you can help her get it resolved right away. Is that okay with you"?

I nodded and mumbled, "Yes," trying not to sound too eager.

"Thank you for understanding," she said. "We will continue the onboarding later." She handed me her business card. "If you have any questions, please call me."

I stood up and whispered, "Thanks," and felt almost grateful for whatever crisis was so severe that Megan pulled me from this before I expired from bureaucratic overload.

I stepped into the hall and closed the door behind me. Shaking Megan's hand, I smiled and said, "Thank you for rescuing me. I thought I was going to be filling out forms for the rest of my life."

Megan tried to smile, but it was more of a grimace than excitement. If her bloodshot eyes and the enormous cup of coffee she carried weren't clear enough signs, her rasping voice made it clear she had been flailing at this for a while. "After understanding why, you may feel a little different."

"What do you mean"?

"Our new CRM app, 'Asgard', was deployed into production Saturday night/Sunday morning. Its success is essential to the business achieving its revenue and growth goals. We stood it up in our normal maintenance window during third shift. Everything started out fine. All of the post implementation verification checks showed it was working as expected. Even the business checked it out and said it was okay. We sent everyone home on schedule. I'd hoped it meant that the additional development testing we were doing had put an end to our struggles with the entire release process."

Megan's phone buzzed. "Excuse me," she said, checking the caller ID. "I need to take this."

Megan tapped her earpiece and took a big gulp of coffee. "Hi. Where are you? Okay, I'm with Chris over in HR. Why don't you get over here so I'm not repeating myself"?

"Sorry for the disruption," she said and took another swig of coffee. She spewed out her words in that chopped hyper cadence you see from people who have had not quite enough coffee to heighten their alertness, but too much to let their thoughts catch up with their mouth before speaking.

"The service desk got a few calls 20 minutes later, mostly about confusion on the new interfaces and functionality ... the kind of thing one always encounters with new releases and deals with under emergency care," she said. "But by the 30 minute mark that trickle of calls became a tsunami that would not stop. And this was on a Sunday. Our CEO called me at the 40 minute mark. I personally took control of trying to halt the damage. It appears ... "

Megan kept talking but I made a mental note. It didn't make sense that they had apparently assigned no one to oversee these issues until the 40 minute mark. That would need to be fixed. Or had there been someone who was coordinating the response? Where was the project manager? Was there an incumbent in my role no one had told me about and that person was still on the job?

Megan interrupted my train of thought. "Chris ... Chris, are you listening to me"?

I nodded as Megan took a huge gulp of coffee.

"This is really important. It appears that while the new app functions reasonably close to the original design, there is an error in the way it stores the data, such that the information recorded is incorrect. And to make matters worse, it also corrupts the data in adjacent elements. It enters bad information and at the same time destroys historical good information. The more it's used, the more it destroys good data already in place. It isn't just keeping us from adding new information, it is also quickly destroying all the good information. As if that weren't enough, as a security and stability feature, the app is designed to immediately archive, so in addition to destroying the live data, it also destroys the backup files ... effectively destroying our ability to perform accurate restores."

2: Where Did My Job Go?

"Well then, it is a good thing that you hired me as the manager of release and deployment," I said. "Don't worry, I've been through situations like this before," I lied. "I am confident I can stop the bleeding and then get to the root cause. If you can just get me in touch with the leaders currently engaged in … "

Megan took another big gulp of coffee and as she pulled the cup down from her mouth, did a half turn and looked down the corridor. I heard footsteps behind me and then a languid, resonant voice … a voice so mellow and relaxed that it sounded just like a summer afternoon in a hammock should feel.

I turned around and walking towards us was someone I had never met before. He was heavily tanned and a little sunburned around the edges. His sun lightened blond hair hung down over his shirt collar and he was unshaven, with about a day's growth of wispy beard struggling to be seen. He had an enormous smile with coffee-stained teeth that looked perfect otherwise, just slightly too big. He was wearing a pair of pressed skinny jeans and a bright yellow polo shirt with a blue dinosaur logo surrounded by the words, "Hell Creek, Montana." He wore heavily scuffed cowboy boots that appeared to have intricate tooling on them.

"Name's Zachary, but that's too many syllables. Just call me Zak … and I'm back."

He chuckled at what he obviously thought was clever. He reached out and shook my hand, then said, "I'm the release and deployment manager. I know you report to me and I'm sorry I didn't get to talk with you before you came onboard but if Megan is good with you, then who am I to disagree? Just follow my lead and you'll do great." Zak paused for a moment and then snickered, "Besides, I was already committed to digging in the dirt in Montana. Couldn't let all those fossilized dino bones escape in the middle of the night, now could I"?

Zak dug through his pockets and produced a textured dark stone about half the size of his fist and handed it to Megan. "I brought this back for you. It's dino coprolite. We dug up tons of it, all fossilized and millions of years old. I thought you might want this as a conversation piece. It should fit perfectly in your office."

I was confused and working up to being really ticked off. This was not how she had presented it to me. Not at all.

I stared straight at Megan, "Could I please have a word with you … in private"?

She never had a chance to answer me. Her phone rang and she instinctively checked the caller ID.

"Oh no," she said and immediately tapped her earpiece on.

"Hi, how is it? …. Oh … "

From that point on, all she did was nod and say either, "Yes," "Okay," or "I understand." I even thought I could hear someone yelling at her over the phone, so loudly that the words were leaking out into the hall. I couldn't understand them, but the fact I could tell she was being yelled at was not a good sign.

After a few moments, she touched her earpiece off and closed her eyes for a moment. The three of us stood there silently in the hall for a moment. Megan spoke first.

"I've got to go and meet with our VP of sales. The CEO was on the call and they were aligned and took turns yelling at me."

2: Where Did My Job Go?

"Can the two of us speak for a moment before you go"? I asked, hoping to understand better what was happening, especially who Zak was and what his role was relative to mine. That fact that the company was struggling at the moment was bad, but in my own internal calculus the situation with me was far more important.

"No. Sorry Chris, but my upcoming ritual evisceration in front of the CEO takes priority. Just handle it. Zak will show you the ropes. He's in charge. But I can tell you one of the things the CEO wants is an assessment of what caused the problem with Asgard and what steps will be taken to ensure it doesn't happen again, because we must get that app running ... but this time without destroying all the company's data."

Megan paused for a moment and then added, "Oh, and they need it before Friday, when they return from their executive offsite in Singapore," before scurrying down the hall.

So executive leadership was looking for an assessment of the company's current and proposed release and post-release support processes. Was it a reasonable timeframe? No. Did I have any input into what was a reasonable timeframe to deliver? No. Were there particular areas of focus they wanted to understand? No idea. Were they available to provide input? No.

It always amazed me how clueless some leaders were when assigning work to individuals. And it always seemed like the higher you went, the worse it got. It was as if they had forgotten what it was like to be on the delivery end of management requests. But maybe it was my problem. Maybe I was the crinkle in the chain of command.

I had this guiding principle I called, "The Rule of Threes." When asking someone to do something, I always gave them three things: WHAT I wanted them to do, If I cared, HOW it was done, and WHY it needed to be done. I did it because that was the way I liked to be assigned work. Clearly, if you needed someone to do something, you needed to tell them what it was you wanted. And if you were concerned they might not know the way to do it, or wanted to micro-manage their activities, then you would tell them the specific steps they should follow to complete it. Most leaders got those two. But too many seemed to always miss the third one – the WHY.

Imagine we were in a dimly lit room and I said, "Open the door" or "Open the door by turning the door knob one half turn to the right and pushing." You could execute the task with "What" and "How." But if I added the "Why," "Because the floor is covered with poisonous snakes and custodians are about to lock the door from the outside," you would be more adaptive and provide a better response. It would allow you to, "Adapt, Improvise, Overcome."

I know when I've talked to leaders about it in the past … trying to give them feedback to improve our working relationship … they usually responded one of two ways. Either I didn't have the scope of vision in my role to understand why it was important, or else I shouldn't be so insubordinate as to question the requests of my leaders. I only needed to execute them. I often suspected that there was a third reason … one they would never admit … that they were clueless about the "Why" and were too afraid to ask their leader about it.

As Megan disappeared, Zak slapped me slightly too hard on the back and said, "This may look pretty grim, it being your first day here at the mothership." He paused and then laughed. "But it happens every time we stand up a new app." Zak pointed down hall in the other direction. "I know the drill well. In fact, we've gotten quite good at back-outs. Don't worry about that right now. Asgard got backed out right after the CEO called on Sunday. So we're going to go see one of the princes of the realm."

As we started down the hall, Zak added, "And don't worry about not knowing what to do. Just shadow me for now and follow my lead. If Megan hired you, then you are probably smart enough to catch on quick."

"Where have you been? I've been interviewing for weeks and this is the first we meet"? I was annoyed and it showed.

"Did you miss that? Like I said to Megan, I was on vacation … out in Montana."

"Montana"?

"Yeah … digging in the dirt out in Montana." He tugged at the logo on his shirt. "But you gotta pay more attention, Chris. Otherwise someone will think you're a real nitwit."

"I'll tell you all about Montana when we get back," said Zak. "But right now we're going to a meeting with the big guy … Madhu."

I gave out a quiet sigh. Looks like I was going to have company whether I wanted it or not.

Knowledge that would have helped Chris

- Because of legal, competitive and operational concerns by human resources, hiring managers and the company's legal department, you will, at best, get a watered-down summary with varying degrees of detail. While you may get more details as part of a statement of work in a contractor/consultant relationship, they will still work very hard to leave as much wiggle-room air between what they really want and what it says. So unless you are an executive under an employment contract, the job you are offered is subject to modification at any time, even on day one.
- Only the best managers understand the need to hire people smarter than they are ... that their role is not to be the smartest person in the room. Their role is to be the coach who assembles a group of superstars and weaves them into a powerful team. It requires them to be confident, self-assured and willing to trust the opinions of those they hire over their own. You will not find these people often, but when you do, stick with them.
- You will not get to pick the other people on your team. Often, you will not be able to pick your immediate manager, just as you don't get to pick their leaders above them. Look hard for areas of commonality, spaces you can share and build on.

CHAPTER 3: FINANCE – WISDOM OR INDIFFERENCE?

Madhu stood with his back to us, scribbling something illegible on a whiteboard that ran the full length of the wall behind the desk in his office. He was completely oblivious to my knock on his open door.

He was the first person I'd seen at the company wearing a suit. It was wrinkled grey wool with a white shirt that looked like he had slept in it for a week. Leather suspenders hung loosely down from his shoulders and were apparently strictly sartorial decorations, as they played no role in keeping his pants from sagging. His suit jacket was balled up on his chair, while all of the other chairs in the room were stacked with irregular piles of loose papers and bound notebooks. His enormous desk was covered with scattered clumps of documents, obscuring all but the edges of two laptops and a tablet. As we stood there, the muffled sounds of a humming vibration and an impossible to ignore Bollywood ringtone could be heard from somewhere in the piles.

He definitely looked different from any CFO I'd ever seen.

After a moment, Zak walked around to the edge of Madhu's vision and gestured with his hand at the edge of the whiteboard. "Madhu," said Zak. "Should we come back some other time, you look rather busy"?

Madhu stopped and froze for a moment, as if mentally still working the problem on the whiteboard, while trying to speak to us at the same time. It was as if his mind was changing gears and he was stuck midstream.

3: Finance – Wisdom or Indifference?

Zak stepped over and stuck out his hand. "I'm Zachery, but you can call me Zak. And this is my new assistant, Chris. We had an appointment with you to get your input on the situation regarding releases and their operational impacts. Megan, my boss, asked me to come up with some recommendations and I understand you have some thoughts based on your experience that would benefit us all."

Madhu closed his eyes for a moment, as if still trying to disengage himself mentally from the whiteboard, trying to remember what this was about. After what seemed like a long staring silence, he slowly nodded and then quietly, in a squeaky voice said, "Yes ... Yes. Of course." Without looking, he pointed over his shoulder toward the chairs full of papers and said, "Please, sit." There was no gravitas or sense of authority in the tone of his words. He sounded more like a young boy whose voice was beginning to change. With his back still to us, he grabbed the grey suitcoat and looked around the office for a place to put it so he could sit down. Finding no immediate place, he simply dropped the balled-up jacket on top of the piles covering his desk and then lowered himself into his chair.

Zak and I stood silently beside the chairs piled with papers for a bit, until Madhu realized we couldn't sit in them and said, "Sorry. Just move those piles to the floor for now." He smiled and added, "They're my reading for tonight."

There was a moment of silence as we settled into our chairs. Madhu looked at his watch. "So you're the release team? Two people seems like a rather large number for what should be a very simple activity. I hope the company's investment will produce a reduction in disruptions."

He checked his watch and said, "You've got 20 minutes left so I will be direct. Our release process sucks. That's because we have ... excuse me ... had ... an incompetent release manager who couldn't build a release process that works to ... " Madhu paused for a moment, letting his words settle into silence before adding, "... to save her job. A total waste of money. So apparently they have hired you to replace her. But I cannot understand why there is the need to keep Zak and his associated expenses around if Chris has been brought in to do this. Do you really need an assistant? How can you justify your value if you can't do such a simple job by yourself? In all candor, I don't know what Megan was thinking."

"Excuse me," said Zak. "Megan may not have properly communicated to you our functions in this event. I am the senior here. Chris was brought in to support my work, not the other way around."

My thoughts stopped cold. I turned and stared at Zak. My response must have been theatrically obvious, because Madhu immediately gave a small wry smile.

"IImmm ... judging by Chris' reaction, it would seem that Megan apparently has some communications issues in her organization, and there are some unresolved questions as to her organizational structure." He pulled a small spiral bound notebook from his shirt pocket and made a few notes. "Interesting."

He jabbed at the air between us. "But I am not concerned with Megan's ... organizational uniqueness. But I will tell you that I am done being asked to join conference calls at 3 am because the release was hosted by an incompetent release manager. The previous person was all full of reasons why it was not her fault, that it was a bad design, or low quality, or poorly tested. I don't really give a fig. She owned it, just like I own the financial performance of this company," with a slight air of almost menace, he added, "Just like one of you own it. And you get paid to make those issues go away. Don't trouble me with all the details, just let me know when you are done."

When he paused to take a breath, I jumped in. The best way to demonstrate the lead role was mine was to act like it. "I won't give you any explanations as to why there are issues."

"That's what she called them," he snapped. "Explanations are nothing but someone's attempt to slip an excuse in as to why they are not accountable for what happened. Explanations are just excuses tarted up with a college education. There are no explanations that I want to hear."

"Got it." I nodded and scribbled the word pompous beside Madhu's name in my notebook. I wasn't planning on forgetting how he felt, and writing anything at all would make sure he felt I was taking this seriously.

"When I meet new people, especially those with more experience in business," I said respectfully, "I always try to get the benefit of their experience, both at that company and elsewhere during their career. Over the course of your work experience have you encountered situations where there were problems with the release process"?

"Are you telling me it's not obvious to you what is going on"? he squeaked. "Any fool could see what has been going on here."

Madhu seemed to know exactly where I was trying to lead him and wasn't going there. I couldn't tell if he thought I was trying to put something over on him, or if he was just being intentionally obstructionist.

3: Finance – Wisdom or Indifference?

"I'm not here to train you," said Madhu. "You are the specialists. We wouldn't have assigned this to you if we thought you couldn't do it. The question is, do you have the will, the focus, and the persistence to execute? Because anything that's not execution is of no value to us."

Zak was sitting there silent, not even bothering to take notes. I didn't understand why he wasn't trying to stand out, so I seized the opportunity to stand out. "Sir, I have a great deal of relevant experience in this area. I will own the accountability for ensuring we have an end to end release process that is effective, efficient and aligned with the best needs of the business."

Madhu slowly shook his head. "Sounds like a quote from a textbook. Books won't help you when you've been backed into a corner by reality. What are you going to do when reality is out of sync with the book? What about when the business wants something contrary to what the books tell you is best practice? We deal in reality here. That's all the board of directors and the stockholders care about. Being aligned with the theory but losing customers and money, is not something that they are interested in hearing about."

"I understand," I said. "And I hope you appreciate that while I am highly experienced in my field, I have a limited exposure to the specific situations surrounding release breakdowns at this company, whereas you have had to suffer through it all. I just want you to know we will remediate areas you see as gaps. I'm a very practical person. I can assure you now that I will build some recommendations that tightly align with the needs of the business. I wish that you would please think of my question more as one colleague trying to benefit from the greater experience of another colleague."

"You are not my colleague, Chris. And don't ever think you are. You don't have the vision … the scope of understanding … the responsibility and accountability I do." He jabbed a finger at me. "Hundreds of people depend on me and my work for their jobs and their paychecks. I have to decide if collectively they are providing adequate value for all the money we pay them, and if not, what steps we should take next." He waved his hand in an arc … pointing from corner to corner of the room. "All you have to worry about is dragging yourself back into your office and remembering to close the door so no one will see you goofing off. Whereas I must spend my time making the truly difficult decisions. Count yourself lucky if you never have to carry my level of responsibility." He sat back in his chair and paused for a moment. "But in the interest of getting you back to work fixing things sooner and earning your salary, I will give you what appears to be some strongly needed advice."

Madhu stood up and with the palm of his hand wiped off some of the information on the whiteboard, creating a small smudgy spot for him to write. He grabbed a black marker and started to write, but it was dried out to the point of illegibility. With a huff of disgust, he launched the marker on a long arc at the trash almost eight feet away. It dropped in … dead center … nothing but net. He fumbled in the tray at the bottom of the whiteboard and popped open a red marker. It must have been fresh because suddenly I smelled a cherry scent.

Unfortunately, the fresh marker didn't make his writing more legible. Either his handwriting was terrible, or else he was writing in some crypto-shorthand that only he understood. Either was possible. Fortunately, he narrated as he wrote, so I was able to grasp some of his points.

"Release manager …" he turned and pointed at me. "… owns all of this regardless of where the root risk is."

"Root risk"? I'd never heard that term before. I didn't recall it from any of my training or processes I'd worked on before. "What is that"?

Madhu huffed and shook his head. "Use your brain. What does every process, every activity, every project, and everything you do have in it? It has risk … risk in either execution, or in initiating a cascade of other risks to successful execution. The root risk is the starting point for all of those risks that could come into play. Risks may become actualized and initiate untoward events that potentially impact users. Those events that occur as a result of the activated risk are the root cause. You have more root risks than you have root causes. It's only when the risks go against you and happen that they become causes. Think of them as potential errors vs. actualized errors. By understanding the root risks, you can project what root causes you may experience for errors. It's anticipatory vs. reactive. Do you understand"?

I wobbled my head. I couldn't tell if he had no idea what he was talking about and was feeding me a line of nonsense, or if there was validity to what he was saying. I hadn't seen anything like what he was talking about in any of my training or experience.

Madhu sighed. "Okay, I'll make it simpler. Most of what become problems in release and operationalization have their origins early in the lifecycle of products. And what happens early in the lifecycle that has the most impact on a product"?

He extended his hand in my direction, palm up, as if he expected me to put the answer in it.

After a moment of thought, I mumbled, "business requirements"?

Madhu shook his head. "Requirements constantly change. It's naive to think they can be managed as a fixed point. Doesn't matter how you try to freeze them. That's because reality isn't static."

That was not my view of the world. Failing to freeze requirements led to scope creep and that resulted in failure to deliver. But I wasn't going to argue that with him right now.

"That's a great insight," I said. "I know that a lot of training talks about how important it is to lock down requirements, and not just ITSM, project management too. They all talk about how that causes project failures, but you have definitely identified a subtle nuance."

"In one sense they are correct. Unchanging requirements makes it easier to deliver those requirements. So if your goal is to deliver something that meets those requirements – freeze 'em."

"Why would we want to produce something besides the requirements we got from the business? Aren't we here to support them ... to be their partners"?

"Yes, and that means building what they want and need, not what they asked for a long time ago. Reality isn't static. Business needs are constantly changing. So if you want to be able to cover your behind by saying you were just doing what you were asked to do, then focus on frozen requirements. And when you deliver something inadequate, you blame the customer. But if you want to be a real business partner, you've got to change just as fast as reality does."

Madhu put the cap back on the marker and dropped it into the tray at the bottom of the whiteboard before sitting down in his chair.

"That means problems during release and deployment most often are the result of what happened in the requirements gather and application development space. We spend a fortune on them and are clearly not getting our money's worth. I am not going to tell you what to do, but when I was closer to day to day delivery, that was the part I made sure was ready for release and deployment. If it's not ready, nothing will succeed. That's where your dangerous root risk is."

"What about here … at this company? What specifically went wrong with the …"?

Madhu cut me off. "Just ask your predecessor about it." He paused for a moment, then gave me a small smile. "Oh, that's right, you can't. She doesn't work here anymore, does she? Do you think maybe she wasn't smart enough to figure it out herself"?

"Yes, but …"

Madhu nodded. "Okay. Aside from the way all release managers seem to treat requirements, the previous release manager failed because she didn't understand the need to ensure all run books reflected the new release. Of course, if she had ensured people were properly trained on the new release, that would have mitigated the situation, but she failed to cover that too. So when there was an issue, people didn't know what to do and there was no way to switch back to the previous release. She had never heard about planning for the worst. All she did was hope for the best. Personally, I think she was too close to Vlad, the owner of application development, and let him get away with too much."

Madhu looked at his watch and waved me off. "Well, I am sure you can figure out what to do and don't need input from her. Besides, we are way over time. Now if you will excuse me, I have real work to do." He stood up, turned around and picked up a different marker. This one smelled like grape … and began writing on the whiteboard … treating us as if we were no longer there.

It was pretty clear the audience was over. As I stood up, he said without looking at us, "Put those papers back on the chairs so I can find them."

Just as I reached the door, he said, "And get release fixed or I'll be squandering my time having this same conversation with someone else in the very near future. Don't waste any more of my time."

We were just outside Madhu's office when he called to us, "Now go try to earn at least some of all that money we pay you, and give me a reason to stop second guessing Megan's decision making capabilities by hiring you for this role."

Knowledge that would have helped Chris

- When dealing with people with extensive experience you may have discussions with them that weren't covered in your training, or are actually contrary to your training. Do not automatically discard the benefit of their experience just because they call it something different, or it is contrary to what you were taught. Remember that no plan ... no concept ... no theory survives contact with reality.

- Root risk is a helpful concept. Think of it as the inverse of a critical success factor ... a critical failure factor. It is important to be able to identify the risks to achieving your critical success factors. Every root risk can be assigned a probability of occurring and the impact on your critical success factors if it does occur. Meter the effort you place on this activity and focus on the ones with the biggest impact. You will not be able to prevent all risks, you may not be able to even respond to them any faster, but by knowing what they are and the dangers they present to your project, may allow you to make structural changes in the overall process that can help improve your odds of success.

- Make sure you calibrate the feedback you get. Studies have shown that there is almost no limit to the amount of positive feedback people will accept and respond to. (That's not the same as slavish fawning.) But you need to understand what those words really mean. There was a senior political office holder in the US who confused his staff with this for a long time. If he said your work was, "Brilliant," it was time to prepare your resume or improve your game. "Brilliant" was the lowest grade he gave. He had a whole different set of words to describe outstanding performance. Unfortunately the best way to learn this is through observation and experience of how others are treated … and learn it before your work becomes, "Brilliant" in his eyes.

CHAPTER 4: BAD BEGINNINGS

As soon as we were outside of hearing range from Madhu's office, Zak pushed me into a conference room and slammed the door behind us. It was one of those tiny conference rooms with a table much too big for it. And of course they had put in the number of chairs the table could support rather than the number that would fit in the room.

Squeezing around the crowd of chairs, Zak grabbed the nicest looking one and threw himself down into it, plopping his notebook down on the table. He leaned back in the chair, as if somehow by pushing against the wall he could magically make the room expand.

Without warning, his chair collapsed and Zak tumbled onto the carpet. I tried hard not to laugh. It was good to see him stumble. But I managed to keep a straight face while I asked, "You okay"?

"Piece of junk," he snapped. "I should sue them for putting such a defective piece of furniture in here." Regaining his composure, he pointed at a chair near me and said, "Sit."

I stood there staring back at him through a long moment of silence. Eventually he said, "Please sit."

I specifically ignored the chair he pointed to and took a quick survey of my choices. Little gestures meant a lot right now. This was about who was in charge … who set the standards … who owned the process, and I wasn't going to cede it to him that easily.

Every chair was broken in one fashion or another. The room looked like the chair graveyard … the place where old chairs came to die. It was the ubiquitous office game of the company buying the lowest cost chairs they could get away with and not replacing them when they broke. The employees with those broken chairs, being ever resourceful, discretely swapped out their old chair for a less used one in the conference room. If it had only been one or two chairs, it wouldn't be much of an issue. But as time wore on, the broken furniture eventually replaced all of the good furniture in the conference room. Then it became a game of finding a chair that wasn't quite as broken as yours. After all, the facilities team never went from conference room to conference room looking for items in need of repair or replacement. Once ordered and delivered, they were forgotten forever.

I had no desire to take the thrill ride Zak just had, so I found the least damaged chair I could. Its height adjustment was stuck at the lowest level, making me feel like I was eight years old and sitting at the grown-up table. And that made me realize that Zak's chair was stuck all the way up, so he towered over me, with the flicker of a dying fluorescent light illuminating him from behind as if I had been arrested and was being interrogated by the police.

"We need to have a serious conversation," he said.

"Sure," I said, "I think we really need to clear the air." That phrase burned on my lips as I said it, but I figured the best approach was to ensure my position was clear to Zak and then talk to Megan to get everything straightened out. I saw no value in burning any bridges with Zak at this stage. If I had to do that, I would … but not until much later. But I was not going to cede my job to him without a fight.

Leaning back in the chair, I said, "Zak, you seem to be a great guy." I lied. So far he seemed nothing but a flake with the attitude of a child. I could not figure out why the company would keep someone like him around. Once Megan clarified his role and made it clear to both of us that he worked for me, I was going to set him up on a performance improvement plan. And I would make sure it was a plan that he had no realistic chance of completing.

"I think we need to resolve who is responsible and accountable for release management," I said. "I think that is something where we both need to hear the same message from Megan, because it is clear we have not."

Zak didn't even wait for me to finish. "Are you insane"? he asked. "You want to talk about some political nonsense after that conversation you just had with Madhu? Do you have any idea how close you just came to getting summarily fired? Madhu is a freakin' corporate officer. He can have you fired with one phone call."

"I didn't do anything wrong," I insisted. "I explained to him the gaps in his logic and gave him some different points of view. Aren't I allowed to stand up for myself ... especially when I am providing a leader with additional perspective they may not be aware of"?

Zak shook his head. "That is exactly the attitude that will make your tenure here very short. Take it from me. I've been here a long time." Zak paused and took a deep breath. "Look, you seem smart and experienced, so I'm surprised you haven't figured this out already. At this company leaders only very grudgingly give up their misconceptions ... regardless of any facts or opinions you may toss at them. And they have very long memories of those who challenge them. How do you think they got to their position? It wasn't by letting people question them at every turn. Challenge them at your peril, even if you are absolutely correct.

People get let go for telling the truth all the time. Think long and hard about whether or not you would rather be employed or right."

"But isn't that a function of how they provide that information? Don't they get into dangerous territory when they respond in a non-professional way? That's always been my experience. Or are you telling me not to confuse our leaders with the facts ... they've already made up their minds and are simply looking for confirmation they are right"? I asked sarcastically. "And what happens when they are not right"?

Zak laughed. "It doesn't matter. Go look up their salaries in the SEC DEF 14A filings. Then look at your own paycheck. And do the math to convince yourself that the company places so much more value on their contribution over yours that they pay them 30 ... 40 ... 50 times what you make. The customer is always right. And our customer is not the business. Our customer is our leadership. So if they say the sun rises in the west, we let them believe that. As long as we deliver what they ask for, when they need it and how they want it, we're covered. It's a matter of survival."

I couldn't believe what I was hearing. If all leadership wanted was someone to agree with them, why hire me. They could have gotten someone cheaper to do that. It made no sense to me. I leaned over the desk and was about to speak when Zak's phone buzzed and played an air raid siren ringtone ...

He held his hand up. "Hang on for a moment. That's Megan's ringtone."

4: Bad Beginnings

Zak tapped his earpiece. "Hi ... how ya doin? Yeah, he's right here with me now. Uh-huh. Okay, right away."

He tapped the earpiece again to end the call.

"Megan wants to see you. Not me .... not us ... just you. And she wants to see you right away."

I nodded and stood up, grabbing my folder from the desk. Good. Now I was going to have that conversation with her about who was in charge here. I started mentally making up the list of items for Zak's performance improvement plan.

"I'll wait here," said Zak. Tugging at the device around his wrist he said, "I need to finish figuring out my new fitness band."

"Shouldn't you go on without me to the next leader? We don't have a lot of time and there is no reason we can't divide our efforts to cover a lot more ground"? I asked.

Zak shook his head. "You just don't get it, do you"?

Megan's door was open and she was sitting behind her desk, talking on the phone when I arrived. There was a woman sitting with her that I had not met. Something told me I was going to get to meet her very soon and that I might not enjoy it. She was looking though a small folder of documents.

Still talking on the phone, Megan waved me in. By the time I reached her desk she'd hung up the phone.

"Please close the door and have a seat," she said. Gesturing to the only unoccupied chair in the room.

The woman sitting with Megan closed the folder of papers and turned to me. She held out her hand and said, "Hi, my name is Becky."

Megan followed with, "Becky is the head of HR. She is my peer and will be sitting in on our meeting."

"Is this about the forms I didn't get to during orientation this morning"? I asked. I knew that wasn't what it was about. They would never bring this level of leadership firepower into a meeting on just that. I just hoped some conversation would break the tension I could already feel in the room.

I'd never met Becky before. She was dressed almost as casually as a third-shift UNIX engineer. But she wasn't sloppy. Her carefully coordinated and sharply pressed outfit made her look more like a soccer mom in her SUV waiting in line for a coffee to go, before picking up the kids at private school and taking them to their afternoon activities. She had a warm welcoming smile that made her face beam when she looked at you. The overall effect was one of engendering trust in her.

I made a mental note to be extremely cautious of what I said around her. People who presented that kind of soft and welcoming persona had often learned how to use it to their advantage … especially in HR.

Megan leaned across the desk and placed her hands together in front of her, with only fingertips touching. She began gently tapping the tips together in a slow, soft rhythm.

"Chris, we have to have a difficult discussion."

Not good. I knew it was probably going to be a lecture and not a discussion – a one-way directive from her to me. Every time I'd heard that sentence before, it came just before I got fired. Except I'd never been fired on the first day before. Becky turned her chair toward me and took out her pen.

I felt like I was being interrogated. What struck me as unusual was that she took her notes on a yellow legal pad instead of using her tablet, which simply sat on her lap and provided a hard surface to rest her papers on. I guessed that way she had to transcribe them into the data records, which gave her the opportunity to "clarify" anything that had been said. And I was pretty sure there wouldn't be any "clarification" in my favor coming out of this meeting.

Having HR present during a "difficult conversation" with your manager was very bad because HR weren't there to protect your rights. They were there as witnesses and backups for the manager to ensure that everything was done exactly as required by law and in accordance with corporate policies. Their role was to help the company ensure maximum value from the human resources, just as a manufacturing manager works to get maximum value from the factory assets. I had no complaint with them or their role. If it were my company, I'd probably do the same. Although I would have felt better if Becky had at least gone through the formality of asking me whether or not I minded if she took some notes ... not that I'd ever be allowed to see them.

Megan and Becky sat silent for a few moments, letting the silence settle in the room ... a variant on the old, "He who speaks first, loses."

Megan took a deep breath and began. "Chris, this is your first day here, so I cannot reasonably expect you to understand all of the nuances of how our company works. At least not yet. However, it is reasonable for me to expect you to act in a professional and respectful manner when dealing with other employees and customers. And that is especially true when interacting with executive leadership. I will tell you that I am disappointed in the way you have acted so early in your tenure here."

"Was there something specific that I did, or should have done today that created a problem? If there were, I was not aware of it," I asked, watching Becky scribbling on the yellow legal pad.

"I doubt you know this, but Madhu and I are old friends. That's why I suggested to Zak that the two of you go to him first. Madhu and I were in college together. I've known and worked with him most of my professional life. I value my personal and professional relationship with him. So you can imagine I did not appreciate getting yelled at by him on the phone, starting the minute you left his office ... and believe me, that is not something he would do easily, willingly, or without serious provocation. He is a very tolerant and relaxed person. Immediately complaining about you is totally out of character for him."

"Was there something in particular that Zak or I did to cause him concern"? I asked, curious to know what had been so offensive about our meeting.

"Of course you did. Madhu is direct, to the point, and specific. He expects the best from everyone in the company and works tirelessly to give his best. I know what he said to me, but I would prefer you to think about anything that may have happened, or may have been said, that would cause him to need to complain directly to me about you."

I'd played this game before. This was where I was being tested to see if I knew what I had done that she objected to. I'd lose points if I didn't know and didn't admit it to her.

But I'd also lose and be convicted by my own words if I admitted it. I hated these no-win games. It would be so much easier if she'd just tell me what she was upset about and then get on to my punishment.

"As to the content of our conversation, I honestly don't know. We had an open discussion on a number of items. There were a couple where Madhu provided us with excellent insight and a couple where I was able to directly add some value by sharing with him what I had seen other successful companies do when addressing these challenges. But at all times, the explicit and implicit focus of the meeting was to gather additional insight on how we could improve the release process."

I took a deep breath and decided that now was as good a time as any to resolve the Zak issue.

"In terms of why he called you directly, I assume that it is because you have an ongoing and long standing relationship with him ... not to mention that you are my direct manager."

Becky stopped writing and put down her pen. Megan sat back in her chair and stared at me.

After what seemed like forever, Megan spoke. "What do you mean by that"?

"Because I interviewed with you, to work for you, and to fix the release process here. We discussed that during the interview." I paused for a second. Megan and Becky sat emotionless and silent.

"May I be direct and candid for a moment"? I asked the rhetorical question, although I knew it was designed more as a warning than as a request for permission. It was good form, but I couldn't think of a single time that I had asked it and someone said, "No."

I took silence as consent and tried to make the best of the moment. An instant before I began, the thought ran through my head of whether or not I should include this one day adventure here on my resume while looking for my next job or simply ignore it.

"Think about Zak as my manager," I said. "Zak couldn't even bother to be here to interview me or have the interview rescheduled at a time when he was available. Obviously he wasn't very excited about my being here … except perhaps as someone to chat with. And look at Zak. I can tell you right now, after only a few hours, that a big piece of the issue is Zak. He doesn't know anything about release. Worse, he has no experience in managing transformational organizational change in a company."

"I think that is an unfair statement," said Becky. "Zak is well thought of by our business partners, as well as IT leadership, and has been for a number of years."

"Zak can be very charming when he wants to … when he thinks he can use it to his advantage. But when it comes to knowledge about how to release and deploy a new application, he is woefully ignorant. And if you want to talk about the changes people need to make associated with that, he doesn't even understand why it is important to have conversations about it with them."

"I don't care if he knows the technical name and processes for rolling-out our releases. I care that he does it right, without impacting the business," said Megan.

"Megan, you hired me to come here and help fix a dysfunctional process for rolling out new apps. Zak has no concept of how to change the way an organization does things, much less what needs to be changed."

I got up and walked to the whiteboard. I picked up a marker and asked, "May I"?

Megan nodded and I began to draw.

I drew three symbols on the board – a square, a circle and a triangle, in that order. Jabbing at the symbols, I said, "Let me show you what I believe Zak really knows … and understand, this is only after a couple of hours with him."

I stuck my finger in the center of the square. "People are frozen in their current modes of behavior. It's safe, they have a sense of control and their roles are well defined. To move them to a different way of working, you've got to unfreeze them. The challenge is that while we can give them tools to help do this, we can't force them to change."

Becky nodded her head and mumbled, "Yes. Looks like Lewin's change model. You do know that there has been a lot of work on change theory since then"?

"Agreed. At a high enough level, all organizational change looks a lot like the Lewin model, the same way all processes look like the Deming model at a high enough level." I tapped the marker at the second symbol, the circle, and drew an arrow to the triangle on the end. "Then comes the hard part … unfreezing them and taking them on a journey to the new state."

I drew a checkmark in the triangle. "Then they have to refreeze in the new state … a place where they can feel secure and in control. Unfortunately, we can only show them the way. They have to take this step themselves."

Megan nervously checked her watch. "Well, I appreciate your little tutorial, but what is your point, Chris? And how is it relevant to what you did"?

"I accept your judgment that I was too aggressive with Madhu and appreciate the corrective coaching." I didn't for a moment think that Megan was right. There was no question in my mind that my discussion with Madhu was exactly what the company needed if it was ever to fix the release process and it was definitely not insubordinate. "It is my first day and I apologize for my mistake. I hope you will understand that all of my actions were strictly professional – done out of a sense of urgency in trying to fix the current situation and not due to any personal issues."

"Thank you," said Becky. "It's important for people to take ownership of their mistakes. It is the first step towards improvement."

"I'm glad to hear that. Mistakes are how one learns to get better," I said.

Megan was a little more direct. "Let me be very clear about the feedback I received from Madhu. He thought you didn't know what needed to be done, that you were incapable of addressing even some of the smaller issues around release … which he felt were obvious to anyone with any training and experience. He felt you were incapable of leading the meeting and keeping it on track, and that you wasted his time by making him tell you how release should work. In other words, you are incompetent and he raised concerns about my apparent lack of judgment in hiring you."

"But what about Zak"? I protested. "He doesn't seem to know anything about deploying new apps into the environment."

"Zak's name did not come up at all in our conversation," she said. "However, yours was mentioned more than a few times and in some very unflattering ways." She paused for a moment and then added, "I urge you to be cautious in your actions going forward. This incident will be noted in your file. Consider this a verbal warning and the next step will be a written warning with a performance improvement plan. If the behavior continues, the third and final step would be separation from this company."

I nodded and said, "I understand. Thank you for your patience and understanding." The words almost burned as I spoke them. But I was experienced enough to know that you should be very cautious about letting pride get in the way of employment ... especially in a new job.

Megan spoke briskly. "In terms of your organizational relationship with Zak, I appear to have misjudged your level of independence and ability to drive the release process by yourself in this environment. That is my mistake and I will not hold you accountable for that. I am going to keep you as the release manager. However, due to some work changes since you accepted your offer, and more evidence of your skill level, the needs of the business require you to report to Zak, who will be your official manager. He is experienced with the company and can provide you with the day to day corrective support that you seem to need. That relationship will continue until I decide otherwise, based on your demonstrated capabilities and the needs of the business. Do you have any questions"?

I was livid, but it appeared my only alternative was to quit. "To speak plainly, I now report to Zak, not to you? He is my manager, but I am in charge of release and accountable for its performance"?

Megan nodded. "Correct."

"Can we set a timetable for returning to what we discussed in our interview, where I would report directly to you"? I asked.

Becky spoke up. "There is no set timetable," said Becky. She pulled a document from her folder and waved it at me. "Please check your offer letter. You do not have a contractually defined work role, nor do you have a specific manager identified. Your role and your reporting relationship are referred to in the offer as subject to modification based on the needs of the business. I have a copy you may read if you wish."

I shook my head. No. What would be the point?

A few moments later the meeting was over. I stood up and was almost to the door when Megan said, "One more thing …"

I stopped and turned. She looked up from the papers she and Becky were examining and said, "So tell me, Chris. Did I make a mistake in hiring you for this job"?

Knowledge that would have helped Chris

- Be conscious but not fearful of the fact that your leader has relationships with other leaders and SMEs. Some of these may greatly exceed the duration of your relationship with your leader. All other things considered equal, people tend to view the credibility of information proportional to the length of the relationship with them. Companies and their leaders are constantly attempting to evaluate employees and you should always assume that interactions you have with your manager's peers or people further up the organization will result in proactive or reactive feedback to your manager. Don't be surprised by it.
- Realize that different levels of the organization have different meta-roles. For example … Subject Matter Experts (SMEs) develop and execute tactical activities that produce fairly immediate tangible impacts. Supervisors and first line managers structure and control the direction of SME activity and senior leaders make decisions based on information presented to them. Treat each of these constituencies appropriately to their type of activity. Failing to do so will collapse the communication link with them.
- A huge challenge you face in establishing ITSM is the natural desire within companies to assign accountabilities based on functional knowledge domains rather than workflows. ITSM improves customer experience by breaking down the walls between functional knowledge domains so that IT activities can be treated as lifecycles and workflows that span those functional towers. Understand that this is a transformational change for people in IT and requires

individuals to be in positions where they are learners again and not the go-to SME.

CHAPTER 5: REQUIREMENTS – VOICE OF THE BUSINESS

Zak and I sat outside the office of Shallah, the director of business relationship management. From what I'd been told, they had an interesting role here. Their entire organization seemed to be based on the idea that the average IT person should be kept as far as possible away from the business side of the house. They viewed IT people as having zero people skills, no concept of discretion and no ability to speak with non-IT people without haranguing them with waves of brutal and opinionated candor.

We were ten minutes past our meeting start time and she was still doing the same thing she'd been doing when we arrived – chatting with two other people sitting in her office with her. Although I didn't hear the entire conversation, from the few words I could pick out, it seemed a long way from any business dialogue.

It was pretty clear Zak wasn't enjoying waiting and somehow that felt rather satisfying. All week we had been meeting with leaders but never once talked about Megan's direction to me. Every time I brought it up he had some distraction to change the subject. Although judging by Zak's attitude toward me, I was confident she had conveyed at least a summary to him privately.

"Is she ever gonna be done"? asked Zak. He seemed a balanced blend of irritation and fidgety, as if the waiting were a slow torture to his overactive but short attention span. "This is really rude of her."

"Patience. Now you know how people feel when you are late."

"That's completely different. I have reasons, she's just goofing with them in there. She's sucking up all of our day with her playtime. She could do that at home or after we were done. This is just wasted time for us."

Almost on cue, the sound of three people laughing and giggling rolled loudly out of the office, followed by Shallah's visitors. I don't know how Zak managed to make that happen. I guess it was just some of that Zak magic that always seemed to be around him.

Before they could get more than a few feet away, Zak stood up and placed himself squarely in the middle of the open doorway and stared at Shallah – not very culturally correct in any company, especially with a director, but apparently it worked.

"Are you Zak or Chris"? came a voice from inside the room.

Zak said, "I'm Zak."

He started to step into the room, until Shallah held up her palm and said, "Hang on a second, let me just take care of a couple of things first."

Zak immediately halted then gave a theatrical huff, like a truculent child, wanting to ensure you knew they were displeased at not being the center of your attention.

After a brief moment during which Shallah seemed to be doing nothing, she waved us in and added a, "Hurry up." It was almost as if making us wait had nothing to do with her need to perform some activity. Rather, it seemed like a gesture of power and emphasizing to us who was in charge.

She did it because it was a meaningless little act that she could make us do.

Her office had several large floor plants, all arranged by the window and filtering the bright sunlight. There wasn't a standard sitting desk. Instead, she had a compact motorized standing desk … one that allowed its user to raise or lower the height depending on their stature. With no chair behind her desk, she had put a walking treadmill in its place. As we walked in, she was striding in place while accessing something on her computer.

She was a tall woman and judging by the triathlon pictures and trophies on her shelves, extremely fit. Her business suit was highly tailored in a way that professionally emphasized the results of her physical conditioning. Her long black hair was twisted up and skewered in place with a couple of inlaid wooden sticks.

Surprisingly there were tall chairs … stool height, opposite her desk, so that visitors did not have to look up at her when talking and allowing their feet to swing without touching the ground.

Finally, with a wave of her hand and a, "Please come in," Shallah welcomed us into her office.

After climbing on to the tall chairs, Zak began the meeting.

"My name is Zak and this is Chris, who just recently joined the company as support for me in this effort. I've been asked by leadership to assess the current release process and identify why we have difficulty deploying new apps. We would very much appreciate your perspective on what works, what's broken, and your thoughts on how we could improve it."

Shallah said, "My team deals directly with the most important people in IT – our customers ... users ... whatever you want to call them. And I say in IT because our customers are part of IT in every sense of the word. They may not reside in one of our cost centers, but without them, you and I, and everyone else in IT, has no business working here. They are the sole reason we have a job."

"That is so true," said Zak. "I don't think I've ever heard anyone encapsulate IT's purpose so concisely. Usually people talk about technology when speaking about IT and they forget the importance of the business in what we do."

After my last conversation with Megan and the warning she gave me, I decided to follow Zak's lead and go softly in this interview. Zak seemed to have some instinctual survival skills ... and I was envious.

"And your team speaks for the customer"? I asked, on my belief that people in leadership positions seemed to enjoy talking about their teams and areas of control.

"As far as you and the rest of IT is concerned, we ARE the voice of the customer. The words and messages my team provides should be treated as if they came directly from the customer's own mouth," said Shallah. "We are responsible for the relationship with the customer and managing it to maximize the benefit IT provides our customer."

"But how do you deal with the conflicts that must occur when someone outside your group speaks with the customers about their requirements, and then interprets it differently from the way your group does"? asked Zak. "Surely that's happened before, and as the senior leader here, you must be involved in resolving those differences so there is no confusion within IT as to what the customer wants"?

Shallah's disposition soured slightly. Her eyes narrowed and her voice dropped to more of a snarl. "Then that would probably be the last insubordinate thing that person ever did at this company. My team is the only group authorized to speak with customers regarding requirements of business need. We are engaged and participate with them in developing their roadmaps, as well as the identification of the tactical and operational leverage needed to achieve those strategic goals."

"Are the members of IT functional teams fully aware of this"? asked Zak. "Please don't misunderstand. I get why you want the control of the customer relationship, as well as the value you bring to both the customer and IT. But in all honesty, no one ever told me this before and so I am wondering how extensively the message has been distributed"?

Shallah snapped back almost instantly. "A document of procedure is distributed to all managers annually. If your manager did not read it, understand it, failed to communicate it to you, or if you weren't paying attention when they did, it is not our problem. Ignorance is no excuse. You may be too IT focused to realize this, but there is serious tension between IT and our business partners. That relationship needs to be handled by people who understand how to keep it from degrading further and ultimately improving it."

"Please excuse us," I said. "Obviously we are ignorant of quite a few things. That is why we are here. The only good thing about ignorance is that it can be cured and we are hoping that you will be kind enough to help us get better. I mean, the relationship with the business must have been really bad when you started. How long has the relationship been adversarial? How far has your team been able to lower the tension"?

It was the wrong thing to say and was said in the wrong way.

Shallah's face tightened up as if she had just sucked on a lemon. "Don't be insubordinate about things of which you are grossly ignorant. And don't ever even imply that my team is not covering for all the inadequacies and fails of the entire IT organization ... especially what we release, or fail to release into the production environment. We take the heat – from the customers and from IT. We provide people like you with cover for their shortcomings. All we ask in return is a little respect and an occasional, 'Thank You.'"

"But we do appreciate all that your team does," I offered. "That's a given and that is why we want to understand more about your team's role in release and deployment as practiced in this company."

"I resent that," snapped Shallah. "You are implying that somehow we are responsible for the deployment failures that have plagued this company."

"No ... not at ... " started Zak. For a moment it felt like he was trying to keep me from another Madhu moment, but she cut him off.

"We provide the requirements from the customer to you. After that, the onus is on you. We do the hard part ... we gather, interpret and freeze the requirements. All you have to do is execute ... or at least try to execute a solution and provide it back to the customer."

"You freeze the customer requirements at a point in time"? asked Zak. "But what happens if the needs of the business change between the time the requirements are given to us and we deliver the solution? How does that information get passed on to IT"?

Shallah shook her head. "Floating requirements are a sign of failure in my team. It's sloppy and incomplete work. Customer requirements must be collected, corrected and locked down tight. Even a far better IT team could not be expected to hit a moving set of requirements on a regular basis. Certainty is the solution."

Zak looked a little confused. Certainty was definitely not his style. "And if the business environment external to the company changes ... say a new product is introduced unexpectedly by a competitor ...""?

"Then we will get those requirements during the next upgrade cycle. We cannot afford the luxury of being dynamic when it comes to what the business needs," said Shallah. "Besides, they almost never know what they need. They only know what they want. Buyers are liars and that is especially true of our customers. We take what they say and from that determine what they really need ... what's best for them and submit those requirements. You can't expect some business owner to really understand, or be able to articulate, what IT capabilities they want or really need."

This seemed like old-school inside-out IT and not outside-in service delivery to me. I didn't think any company was still that old-school, so I asked a question to clarify if I understood her right.

"So you don't give us their direct requests. You give us your interpretation of them. How do you know you understand what they are saying? Is there ever any conflict when the results are produced"?

"Of course we have to educate them on why the solution we selected is the best one for them, but you have to remember that while they may know their business, they are woefully ignorant of what technology can and should do. You would not believe the requests we get because some sales manager read an article in a magazine during an airplane ride. They have no concept of sustainability and supportability. I mean, they don't even know what the overall technology roadmap looks like. How uninformed can you get"?

"Do you have a lot of deep technical knowledge in your team … people that may have been SMEs and are trying to work their careers into more of the business side of the company"? I asked.

"It's not necessary," said Shallah. "What we do is much more of a managerial function and as we have consistently proven, a good manager can manage anything, so our team members are more than up to the task of working with people on the business side who are so technically illiterate."

Shallah gave a little chuckle and said, "In the company of the ignorant, even the technically weakest newb is a techno wizard."

"Wouldn't it help if we just go and talk to the requesting business units themselves"? asked Zak.

"You know," I added, "Bring the requestor as close as possible to the people providing the service, as a way to reduce the possibilities of miscommunication."

Shallah's eye's narrowed as she looked squarely at me. "Do that and it will be the last insubordinate thing you do."

There was no doubt that Shallah meant it.

Knowledge that would have helped Chris

- Business requirements are the starting point and core of a successful release and deployment process. In the ITSM request based world, IT's focus is on providing capabilities to the business to help them better achieve the company's goals. Misalignment of those requirements ensures a failure in the deployment, regardless of work done downstream.

- IT must ensure the collected requirements accurately map the business need, or IT will create a release that does the wrong thing right if they do not include all of the functional capabilities the business needs. In a similar fashion, failure to monitor the performance of the new capability will make it impossible to determine if it is properly addressing the business need.

- Gathering requirements from the business in a way they can be best used to deliver the right solution is a challenge. The introduction of service based IT changed the focus from inside-out to outside-in … from IT deciding what the business needed and then building it, to the business deciding what they needed and IT providing that capability. However, this means that IT must now react as fast as, or faster than the business, in response to the changing business environment. The business requirement today may be obsolete and superseded by new requirements before IT finishes deployment, if IT takes too long. The solution is to parse

---

the needed capabilities into smaller elements that can be quickly delivered in a more agile way.

- Don't be afraid of having a "Big Tent" approach to requirements, or of having the business customer deeply involved in design and testing phases. The more involved people are in making, seeing, or participating in the decisions being made, the more ownership they feel for them. Never gather the requirements and then hide in a corner until the solution is deployed. That creates unpleasant surprises.

CHAPTER 6: SALES – HEART OF THE BUSINESS

The traffic on the way to work was terrible. Four lanes of interstate all going about two miles an hour. I'd relied on the mapping program to find me a shorter way to work but it turned out yesterday had been one of those half-holidays where the government, schools and banks were the only things closed. It created travel more consistent with a Saturday than a weekday. But now things were back to normal and I was getting the full impact of what my commute would be on this route on normal days.

I hated traffic … really hated it. And while I wished accidents or tragedy on no one, it really infuriated me to finally get through a stall and crawl section of highway without seeing any reason why we'd just spent 20 minutes traveling two miles. Congestion slowed things down for no good reason other than too many people were trying to use a road that wasn't big enough to accommodate the traffic when it was first opened, much less ten years later. And now I was on a bumper to bumper four lane highway heading to work, and no one was moving faster than five miles per hour, while the speed limit was 65 miles per hour. Cars stretched to my visual horizon in both directions.

I was succumbing to the hypnotizing effect of traffic crawl when an expensive blue sedan crossed two lanes and forced me to slam on my brakes to avoid hitting him, as he intimidated his way into a gap insufficient for a car half his size. My tires screeched in complaint. Furious, I leaned on the horn and cursed at him to go back to the Autobahn his car had obviously been designed for. I yelled instructions about the impossible things he should do to himself before waving my hand at him using the single finger salute of good friendship.

The fact that he waved the same salute back only infuriated me more.

That was when the realization hit me. I had been working on trying to structure a new process based on release oriented activities that required a variety of capabilities, from people relationships to quantitative analysis. It was a broad range of skill sets. It had to be.

Release is a lot more than just the act of deployment into production. Release is a long lifecycle process that touches most of the steps involved in creation or remediation. It first gets alerted back when an item is proactively or reactively identified and can extend from the service desk through to a post implementation review. That means it requires the actions of a variety of people, many of whom have different skill sets and orientations – observe and report, diagnose and design, or build and implement, to name a few. No one person has a strong focus in each area. That's why they are different roles.

When I was designing a revised release process, I'd simply lifted the roles straight from the best practices documentation. But the problem was, best practices implicitly assumed you always had plenty of people, with one who was the right match for each role, or at least that anybody could step into any role. But reality is quite different. I was trying to think of people who could fit into the pre-defined roles. Perhaps that was wrong. Perhaps the way to solve this was to understand who could do what and then restructure the roles outside of best practice, in order to make the best use of everyone … like a coach on a sports team. My mind was racing with possibilities. I was so excited about the idea that I was actually looking forward to seeing Zak so I could share the idea with him.

Zak was waiting in my cube for me when I finally arrived. He was sitting in my chair with his feet propped up on the inverted recycling container … earbuds in his head, fussing with the activity tracker on his wrist and trying to sync it to the tablet nestled on his lap. I wondered how long he'd been sitting there doing nothing. He may have been my so-called boss for the moment and he may have been an employee who had been here longer than I had, but so far, I remained unimpressed.

"Am I disturbing you or do you want some help"? I offered sarcastically as I tossed my folio down onto the desk.

"Thanks … I'll figure it out," he said without looking up. He waved his tracker in the air while tapping his tablet. "Says I walked over 48,000 steps since this morning. Can't be right. It's my second replacement. I must have not initialized it properly, or else I'm double counting with the data from the old one. This one came yesterday and it seems just as defective as the last one. But I'm not giving up again. I'll get it. Just takes a little time."

Shaking my head, I sat down across the desk from him. It was interesting to see my cube from the visitors' side. I made a mental note to put some things behind my chair that would be an appropriate background to give people a visual message of how I wanted them to view me.

As I sat there, Zak continued to ignore me. He never moved, so I leaned over and jerked the tablet out of his hands, popping the earbuds connection out of the tablet.

Zak yelped and spun around to face me. "Hey! That was cruel and uncalled for. Why did you do that? Did you lose my data? I ..."

"Wasn't it you who told me something to the effect that I needed to think about my priorities"? I said.

Jobs were not that easy to find, I told myself, and I needed to recognize that I was very fortunate to have this one, even if they had changed the rules on me and I was working for someone who had no idea what he was doing.

"If, under the pressure of all the critical issues you are managing, you forgot," I said. "We have a meeting scheduled with Juan, the head sales guy. You know, the one who has been chewing on Megan about the deployment failures and has the CEO's ear. Or perhaps you would prefer me to handle it myself while you continue these critical managerial tasks"?

Zak looked at me and laughed. "Sarcasm, my friend, is a very ugly thing. I'm okay with it just between us in private, but there are a lot people here who would view it as insubordinate and having an attitude that is contrary to our company's culture. It's up to you, but assuming that trip to Megan's office yesterday wasn't so she could show you her vacation photos, I'd work very hard to make sure I didn't cross any lines if I wanted to stay around."

I guessed that was Zak's idea of a professional warning or threat of some kind. It was hard for me to tell whether the things that came out of his mouth were serious or not.

Zak got up from my chair and headed for the door. "I'm just saying," he said before adding, "You hungry? We've got a little bit of time before we are due to meet with Juan. I know of a food truck not too far away that has an amazing banh-mi breakfast sandwich. I have it every day with a jumbo café-da. It winds me up better than a six-pack of energy drinks ... really makes me productive. You'll love it. I'll even drive."

To be productive, I thought. That's a giggle. I would love to see Zak being productive ... at anything besides goofing off.

Juan, the VP of sales and marketing, was standing outside his office, speaking with his administrative assistant when we arrived. He wore a perfectly tailored business casual look. His navy blue blazer had a soft roll of the collar and the actual buttonholes for the gold buttons on the sleeves made it appear to be at least custom, perhaps even a bespoke piece of tailoring. A pocket square with the pointed ends up poked out of the blazer's breast pocket. Its faint pastel shade perfectly complemented the color of his shirt.

His shirt looked hand-stitched and was open at the collar. A heavy gold watch hung from his left wrist. With a precise haircut and broad smile, he looked like an ad from a fashion consultant – warm and welcoming, understated but impressive to those in the know. He radiated an impression of professional and authoritative – an iron fist inside a velvet glove. The epitome of dressing like your next job in a large corporate environment, although he already made more money than the CEO.

His look had impact and style. It grabbed your attention and made him memorable. Initially, I wondered if his look had been something of his own design or was the product of professional image guidance. Putting your image together like this was the kind of skill necessary to succeed at his level. But at the same time, the more I saw, the more his

look, while powerful, started to seem very old-school …
something you'd see ten years ago. The senior leaders I'd
seen lately were not so focused on standard corporate style.
Instead, each of them had their own individual flavor. They
still had classic style, but the focus seemed more on being
creatively and uniquely individual. I just didn't see it.

Juan's office was understated for what I had come to expect
from the head of sales. Usually it was decorated in a brash
way to show the success and power of the occupant … the
achievements they'd accomplished … the trophies they'd
bagged for the success of the company and the benefit of
their wallet.

His office was minimalist. Still executive level, but exuding
Zen-like calm. You could almost feel the stress draining
away as you stood within it.

There was only a carved wooden desk with a couple of
high-backed leather winged chairs directly in front of it for
guests. But minimal didn't mean like the kind of square
footage I worked in. The room was probably 200 square
feet with an enormous floor to ceiling window overlooking
the adjacent forest preserve. There was no harsh fluorescent
lighting anywhere – only illumination that was soft and
easy on the eyes.

The furnishings were all much better than anything I had
ever even considered for my house, much less aspired to in
an office. The walls were covered by a subtly textured
wallpaper done in a light pastel green and sand pattern. It
looked like it was actually silk, but I was too intimidated to
actually walk up and touch it … secretly hoping that Zak,
and his unrepressed persona, would have no concern about
wiping his hands on it and then adding some inappropriate
comment. The wall covering was set off by an intricate and

complementary colored Persian rug that occupied most of the floor. There were no bookcases ... no filing cabinets ... no storage space of any kind visible. There weren't even any papers on the desk, just an older desktop computer, two tablets and three phones. Against the back wall I could see the outline of what appeared to be a hidden door. My mind began reeling off all the things that could be behind that door. Interestingly enough, there were no chairs opposite his at the desk. Instead, there were four chairs arranged in a diamond and facing each other over by the window. The weekly cleaning bill alone for this room must have been more than the total cost to outfit my cube and kit me up with technology.

Juan looked like he was going to be a person of interesting complexity. The biggest surprise was that there were none of the usual awards, certificates and selfies with important people that usually peppered the walls of a sales executive.

However, there were two distinctive and different touches of personality in the room. One was a jali openwork style carving in kadam wood of four elephants arranged in a line trunk to tail, that looked like they were marching along the edge of the desk, subtly separating his personal space from guests. The other was a spot-lit display of five antique pachinko machines on the wall opposite the large polarized window.

Zak immediately walked over to the wall display and began examining one of the machines. Before I could say anything, he began playing it, sending balls arcing and bells ringing inside the box.

"Is this working okay now"? he asked.

Juan nodded. "If you say so. I don't really play them. I'm interested in having them restored to working condition, but I appreciate them for the amazing works of art they are. Without your help, I doubt that particular one would ever have been good enough for me to hang on my wall. Are you sure I can't pay you for your time? I know you had to make some parts for it and that must have taken time and expense."

Zak shook his head. "I enjoy bringing them back to life and it lets me spend time with machines I could never afford. As long as you let me play with them every once in a while, I'm good."

"That's fine by me," chuckled Juan. "I don't play them. I just like the way they look. Besides, if you break anything, I know you will fix it."

He turned to me and said, "Juan somehow found out I really get off on restoring antique mechanical gambling and amusement machines. This one was a very cool challenge. It was nothing more than a wall hanger parts machine when I got it, but now it's restored to as good as new."

I had to admit there was something about Zak that was ingratiating and charming about him that seemed to sit very well with more than a few people.

Juan walked over to the four chairs by the window. They were arranged facing each other, but with no tables or other surfaces around them. Just a conversation area. He sat in the chair that left his back to the room and gave him an unobstructed view of the forest preserve. He motioned for us to join him.

Juan settled into his chair and slowly crossed his legs. As he picked a bit of lint from his trousers, he said, "Tell me Zak, have you recovered from our boat trip"?

"Boat trip"? I asked.

He looked straight at me and said, "You must be Chris. I'd heard you were coming to take some of the load off of Zak so he can focus on fixing our stability issues."

Zak interrupted and turned to me. "Juan owns a new trimaran and I've been helping by crewing for him while he gets comfortable with it before he and his wife take it down the coast this summer." Zak smiled at Juan. "And who knows, maybe if he likes my work, he'll take me on the trip to help out and give him more free time."

"As long as you remember who the captain is," chuckled Juan.

"Aye-aye, sir," said Zak with a chuckle.

"Perhaps you would like to consider working as crew on my ship," said Juan. "We can always use an extra hand. Although you will need to put some more time in at the gym." Juan paused for a moment, then added, "I'm not saying that you need to lose a few or could be in better shape. Everybody could benefit from more time at the gym. I'm just saying that the way we sail is unlike anything you have seen. No motorized winches here. It's a pretty intense aerobic workout."

He pointed at Zak. "How often do I hit the gym"?

"I know you do a 90 minute spinning class, five nights a week, because I'm in that same class," said Zak. "And I can hardly keep up with you."

"And I'm ten years older than you," laughed Juan. "But that's because you don't do the morning routine I do three mornings a week before I get here. I do two spinning sessions, alternating with free weight sessions."

Juan turned back to me. "But don't worry about it for the first time. Try it out. There is no shame in not being able to keep up. If you can't cut it, we'll just put you to work washing the hull or something more in line with your abilities. After a shakeout sail, you can decide if you have the commitment it takes to step up."

"Thanks," I mumbled. "I really appreciate your offer and your faith in me."

"Faith has nothing to do with it," said Juan. "I'm giving you a chance to run with the big dogs. Either you've got it or you don't."

Juan shifted in his chair and said, "Well, shall we get to the matter at hand? I don't want to run out of time before we even get started."

Zak spoke first. "I'm trying to identify recommendations for how we can improve the release and deployment process. I'm looking for feedback from those most directly impacted by any failures in that process. I'm sure you are aware of some of the recent challenges that have arisen during the transition into operations. Leadership realized the importance, scope and need for a speedy resolution. That's why they brought Chris onboard to help me in that effort. The most recent release, Asgard, has had significant impact on you and your organization, so it seemed appropriate to gather any insight or concerns you have."

Juan pointed out the window. "Turn around and look out the window. It's really beautiful and peaceful outside. From here it looks the bucolic embodiment of nature in perfect balance ... calm, orderly and at peace."

"Yep." Zak and I both nodded.

"Looks can be deceiving. It is in fact a war zone. There is constant competition by plants and animals for supremacy ... all fighting for existence and the ability to continue. And when one competitor is vanquished, five more spring up to take its place. Those organisms that cannot respond or compete are quickly swept aside. They are the losers of history. Survival belongs to the strongest, the fastest and the wisest."

Juan shifted slightly in his chair. "So it is in business. Do not be misled. We are in a constant state of total warfare against an unending sea of competitors ... any one of which would do anything ... anything at all ... to steal our business and grind us into the dust of history. My job is to prevent that from happening and to turn the tables on them ... to destroy them so we can succeed. My business is selling, just as yours is IT. While my role is to bring in revenue for the company to support everyone from board members to stockholders, yours is to provide tools that leverage my efforts and make my team more effective. Without me, there is no reason for your entire organization to exist. I pay for all of you, as well as the tools you provide me. As long as it gives me an edge over my competitors, I'm happy to do so. I will tolerate almost anything except failure."

Juan paused for a moment, then leaned forward towards us, his forearms resting on his thighs. "My request of IT is very simple. Above all else, do not break anything that is currently working. And if you provide me with new tools, make sure they are ready for prime time and can withstand the volume of business my team generates. Is that such an unreasonable request"?

"Of course not," said Zak. "We realize that without your team, there is no company. Our job is to help you achieve your goals. That's why we are here."

Juan sat back in his chair and crossed his legs again. He straightened the crease in his trousers before looking directly at Zak. He was definitely not smiling.

"In the interest of time, let me be direct. To even the most naive observer, IT seems incapable of producing and delivering requested solutions on time and on budget that are both fit for purpose and fit for use. If IT were an employee, they'd have been on a performance improvement plan a long time ago, and would have been fired by now. It's not personal. It is strictly business. Right now, IT is as severe a challenge for my team to overcome as any competitor in the marketplace. If I were the CEO I would have outsourced the entire group of ..."

Juan paused in almost a melodramatic fashion ... searching for the right word.

"Shall we say ... individuals ... we call IT to an organization that could deliver on their promises and support the company. And I have been quite direct in expressing that thought to Megan."

Since I worked for Zak, I didn't have to worry about that message being directed at me. Zak was senior and therefore he owned the accountability for the deployment of solutions. For the moment I felt comfortable, I was not in danger of being tossed under the bus that my designated manager was the poor devil holding that ticket.

To Zak's credit, he appeared to handle the message well. He didn't seem to take it personally. And unless he called on me, I was going to let him be the center of attention.

"Thank you for that frank assessment, Juan," said Zak. "I appreciate the seriousness of the situation and am grateful for the candor of your assessment. As I am sure you understand, organizations that move to an outsourcing model go through some wrenching changes that can be even more damaging to their business model than stumbles during deployments. Can you aid our efforts at continual improvement by offering some input as to where you think the remediation focus should be while using the existing IT organization"?

Juan nodded. "The root of the problem is that IT is not preparing people for the new solution. The training is terrible. Have you ever seen an engineer trying to train a group of sales people on a new product? It's pitiful ... like a fish trying to teach a dog to talk. IT is either too clueless or too cheap to do it right. Training on company offerings is one of the best investments we as an organization can make. And the training you make available for our customers on the upgrades and new products is embarrassing. For many of the updates there is no training available ... at any price. Do you think the best and highest use of the revenue producers on my team is for them to design and deliver training? Every IT person ought to be required to work in sales for a year to understand how a business operates and how what they do impacts us all."

"This company is not here to produce IT," said Juan, his voice calm, unwavering ... the tone of someone who is well accustomed to holding all of the cards. "IT is here to leverage the capabilities of the people bringing in the revenue and servicing our customers. If it is impossible to hold IT accountable for their performance and their activities are not part of our core competencies, then the obvious solution is to turn the function over to a third party who is more experienced and can be held accountable for their performance via contractual payments."

"Yes," I offered. "But as Zak suggested, it is an extreme and very disruptive solution. It is not …"

Juan cut me off. "Is it less disruptive than having solutions fail at the most inopportune times? Is it less disruptive than the revenue that is lost because of the repeated failures? Is it less disruptive than the loss of long term customers because of it? I know because I see the cost to the company every time IT fails. I am tired of wasting my time doing that. I've already floated the idea to my peers and my boss and will present my proposal to the board of directors at their upcoming meeting."

"Yeah," said Zak. "But even to consider going down that road will take some time. After all, candidates to perform the IT functions would have to be vetted."

"With all respect, Zak," said Juan. "That is not your concern. However, I have been in the industry for many years and have a great many people in my network. I have already prepared a short list with recommendations for the board. Being successful means knowing how to move faster than the next guy. I happen to know someone whose outsourcing firm would be an excellent match for us from a delivery and cultural standpoint. Unfortunately, they don't take on the former IT people, they use their existing employees."

"That's harsh," said Zak. "After all the time those in IT have given the company… "

"For which they were paid. If any of them feel they aren't loved enough then they should go get a dog, because our stockholders pay for performance and our obligations are to those stockholders, not the employees."

"We really appreciate your candor, Juan," I said. "However, we still would like to prove to you that we can do it. Are there some specifics of things you find especially critical to mitigating this situation? How can we help you feel better about IT and our performance"?

Juan glanced at his watch and stood up. "I have to leave, but I can briefly address your question. Every business process has a lifecycle to it. Our sales are primarily consultative sales and they have a lengthy lifecycle to them that even the greenest of sales reps knows and lives every day. So I can tell you what you need to be doing, even though I am not an expert in your field."

Juan walked to his desk and pulled two phones from his drawers. He slipped them into his pockets and picked up a thin leather folio. "Suppose you are my customer. I come to you and get your requirements. I design a solution. I get your okay on the solution design. I assemble the solution, test it and when I am convinced it is good, I train your team on it. I make sure your team is trained on it because giving you a solution without you knowing how to best use it is like giving a microwave oven to a bear. It won't add to their capabilities, but it will really tick them off. And once you are trained well, I work with you to launch it appropriately into your environment, while giving you extra support in the beginning to make sure all goes well."

Juan walked around the desk toward the door. "It is just that simple. It's the same model we use for everything we do. That's why a good manager can manage anything. They understand the universality of lifecycles. That's why any of my sales managers could manage the release process much better than IT does."

I started to speak, "But what would you have us do specifically that would ..."?

Juan stopped in the doorway and slowly shook his head. "Don't break things that work and deliver things that do work. In other words, perform. The only thing that IT can do to make me feel better about its performance is for it to perform. How you do it doesn't matter to me. Performance is the only thing I count. If you can't perform, then step aside and let someone else who can do it."

Juan's voice relaxed and he turned to Zak. "By the way, I forgot to tell you, Zak. I have a line on some antique pachinko machines from the 1930s. They're currently wall hangers, but I'm sure you can make them sing. The shipment should arrive here on Friday. I'll show them to you this weekend before we go sailing ... if we're still on for Saturday."

Zak nodded. "I'm looking forward to it."

Juan smiled, turned and walked out the door.

A few seconds later, Juan's administrative assistant came in and said, "Would you mind leaving? I can't leave you alone in his office and I want to lock up. You can go wherever you want. You just can't stay here."

Knowledge that would have helped Chris

- I once asked the VP of sales for a multi-billion dollar company what he thought IT's most important role was … what was the number one thing above all else that we should strive for to provide him with leverage to achieve the company's business goals … where could we add the most value to his organization … what should be our number one priority? His answer was priceless, "Don't break anything that is working."
- Sales brings in most of the company's revenue and pays for most of the company's expenses … including IT. To do this they are intensely focused on delivering results. Within ethical and legal parameters, they are often not interested in the details of how other parts of the company do their work. They are interested in the outputs from other organizations where those deliverables increase or decrease their ability to meet their goals, but not very much on the mechanics behind them. This means the typical sales employee knows as much about how IT works as the typical IT employee knows about sales. The language is different, the focus is different and the personalities tend to be different. That is why IT needs to devote substantial time to building those bridges to their customer's world. As many sales people will tell you, their customer's perceptions are our sales team's reality. They must meet the prospective customers on their own ground. IT must do the same for their customers within the business.
- It is important to be able to separate out personal and professional during conflict situations. Professionals that are extremely results driven, such as successful sales or attorneys, have mastered the skill of remaining friends

with someone despite undergoing an intense business confrontation. To successfully enable ITSM you will need to build strong relationships between business and IT. However, there will be many times where the needs, interests and capabilities become adversarial. If you have built the personal connections you will navigate these successfully.

CHAPTER 7: APPLICATION DEVELOPMENT

Vladimir was the director of application development. He and his team had built most of the applications the company relied on for revenue and to support our own internal activity. His office was almost the antithesis of Juan's. Where Juan's office was understated to the point that one immediately realized the occupant was someone to be both feared and respected, Vladimir's office was loud and brash ... making a noisy statement of overcompensation about his place in the company hierarchy.

One wall of Vladimir's office was tiled with a collection of certificates for every type of technical training I'd ever heard of, and a few that I never knew existed. I half expected to see a certificate from his elementary school teacher congratulating him on his spelling test. Some of the certificates were metallic and mounted on wood backgrounds. Others were merely framed paper, many of which were showing the yellow fade of too many years in the sunlight.

Vladimir had been around for a while. It was unusual for someone to keep old certificates hanging on their wall as trophies, especially a director. I couldn't recall anyone at his level who was so proud of their technical classroom training that they kept all of their old certificates on the wall, or even put any of them on their wall. It was more the type of thing one saw in an SME's cube.

The rest of his office was populated with a parade of old-school geeky toys. A crudely built set of shelves cantilevered from the window frame and contained dozens of solar driven toys ... all moving, but accomplishing nothing other than pointless kinetic frenzy. I wondered if they were there just for the joy of free movement, or perhaps a deeper statement about the difference between activity and results.

Six radiometers were scattered randomly on bookcase shelves, their vanes spinning wildly in the morning light streaming through the window. On the corner of his desk there was a globe magnetically suspended to look as if it were ignoring gravity and spinning slightly out of sync with the radiometers. There was a large red stapler on his desk with the name "Milton" written on a piece of paper and taped to the side. He had a pair of scissors lying on the desk that looked like they had a laser guide attached to them.

Obsessive tech for tech's sake was everywhere. Wherever something could have a bit of tech attached to it … regardless of the usefulness, Vladimir seemed to have it. There was one exception. In a far corner of the room sat a burgundy meditation cushion. Judging by the creases and wear marks in the surface, it was very well used.

Vladimir's office seemed much more like an old-school stereotype of an application developer than a senior IT leader.

That seemed to extend to even Vladimir himself.

He was dressed way below business casual, even for an AppDev team. His hair was closely cut in the khokhol style, with a knot of hair from the top of his head drooping down over his forehead. It was dyed a shade of yellow that seemed three shades beyond anything natural. He wore a faded t-shirt that appeared to have once been imprinted with a logo, but had since been washed into a faded blur of pastel tints. His legs were up, perching a pair of well-worn leather lineman's boots on his desk. Judging by the scuff marks on the surface of the desk, it was not an uncommon position. He wore faded blue jeans, with the blue worn down to the white threads in spots. The jeans were held up by a belt bearing an enormous silver bull riding buckle from some event in Cheyenne, Wyoming. Wires connected to his earbuds hung down and into a shirt pocket. A pair of curved amber tinted Gunnars rested on the end of his nose.

He definitely didn't look the part of ready for promotion to vice president at all. It was almost as if it were a game, that the more non-standard he looked, the more alpha-developer he looked and the better AppDev engineer he must be. But perhaps he was dressing for the position he aspired to – that having had experience in the leadership world, he was hoping to devolve back into a developer. I knew the company thought he must be good at what he did, because otherwise they would not have suffered his eccentric style. It was definitely not the kind of image sales teams would be comfortable sharing with prospective customers.

But I had no problem with how he chose to decorate himself or his environment. I was much more concerned with how he could help us solve the release problem. And for that I was counting on Zak.

Of anyone in a role model position at the company, I hoped that Vladimir would have the most in common with the real Zak … not the fake get-along guy. And maybe … just maybe, Zak could communicate better with him and we could get some great insight. After all, it made a lot of sense to me that even if App/Dev wasn't the source of the problem with failing apps, they were right in the middle and had to be a contributor. If the app wasn't delivering what was required, then it was defective and that was the domain of AppDev. Anybody could see that.

So I was going to let Zak lead on this interview. Besides, it helped me keep a lower profile. I was determined to do everything I could to keep a low profile to minimize the chances I would get booted out of the company anytime soon. Far better it should be Zak than me.

Zak was all smiles when he said, "Vladimir ... can I call you Vlad? I'm Zachary, but you should call me Zak."

Vlad pulled one of his earbuds out. He leaned forward and jabbed a finger at Zak's nose then nodded and grunted.

Zak laughed, so I assumed that they had established a communication link on some deep developer level that I couldn't even begin to understand. But that was okay. I didn't need to understand it, I just needed to be able to benefit from it.

Zak said, "I'm here to get feedback from you on what you think is causing us to have so many issues with deploying the new releases your team builds. There are some people who think the defects must be due to something not happening in your team. Any thoughts"? After a moment, he jerked a thumb in my direction and added, "Chris is my assistant."

Vlad sat up straight in his chair and in a heavy South Boston accent said, "What did you just say? Are you implying we do junk work? When was the last time you went three days with no sleep to get code written for some clueless seat-warmer"?

I jumped in to avoid a conflict that would shut down our information pipeline fast. I turned to Vlad. "Look, I'm sorry we seem to be getting off on the wrong foot here. The fact we're speaking to you is not a reflection of any belief by anyone that AppDev is the source of the issues that have arisen on prior releases. As part of our due diligence, we're just looking for your perspective and your insight into the process."

Vlad laughed and said to Zak, "Your friend here is hilarious. That's more vague nonsense than we ever get from those BRMs. They take forever to get to the point. But that's okay. I'm used to it."

Vlad turned to me, "That's okay, friend. I understand people like you. Trying to be someone you're not is too hard. No one is that good an actor. You've got to be true to who you are."

Vlad looked at Zak. "Don't worry about people accusing me of being a slackard. I've been called worse than that by my own staff ... and in front of my boss, too." He laughed a little too long and a little too loud. "Sometimes when the pressure is on, people get a little hot and loose with their words. Stuff happens and if you get into a froth because someone challenges you, it's time to go home and get your big boy pants on. You must be under some serious management threat to have fuses that short. Just let it out and move on."

I was a little bit surprised at how quickly Vlad flipped from hot to cool. It made me wonder if there was much depth to the feelings he was expressing, or if he was much like Zak ... no filter, no logical construction of thoughts, just a filter free flow of ideas. I was accustomed to a much less tolerate corporate environment. It seemed Zak really did have the ability to know exactly how to approach people and get the most out of them. Now if I could only figure out how to do the same...

"Thanks," said Zak. "We really appreciate your understanding. So what is going on with all these lame apps ending up in production"?

Vlad shrugged his shoulders. "Stuff happens. Nothing is perfect. Nothing lasts and nothing is ever done. If you start trying to make things perfect you will go insane. No one ever gets to the 6th sixth sigma."

I turned back to Vlad. "One of the questions involved you and the QA team. I'd been questioned that maybe the issue was the QA team not working close enough with your team to ensure the appropriate use cases were tested before the application was released ... that perhaps you were developing solid apps but due to issues in testing, there were faults in the integration of what is often incredibly complex applications."

Vlad chuckled and pulled the second earbud out ... tucking both of them into his pocket with his phone. "I can say without question that now the AppDev team and the QA team work closer together here at this company than at any other company ... absolutely."

"That's a very powerful statement. How do you know that"? I asked, as I looked through my notes for the name of the QA leader. "How do you coordinate with ..." I skimmed through the papers until I found the QA leader's name ... the one that Megan had given me. "Got it ... with Mitch"?

"Mitch"? Vlad chuckled a little. "You are way out of date. There have been several since then. Mitch was quite a while ago. But you were here then, Zak. Do you remember Mitch Baptiste"?

Zak laughed. "Who could forget? He went screaming down the hall with the cops and corporate security in hot pursuit."

"Oh, wow. I missed that," said Vlad. "Did anyone grab a video? I did see him getting rolled out strapped down to the gurney … screaming threats and lawsuits at everyone he could think of. I guess that was why they announced he had resigned for medical reasons. I was really glad he didn't work for me. The idea of having to check under my car each day for wires for the next couple of months would be too much. I make it a point never to hire psychos … unless they happen to be really good coders. But they have to be really amazing."

Vlad pulled an old looking organizational chart from his desk drawer and pointed at his name. It was in the AppDev director box and listed as "Acting" in the QA box.

"This was right after they hauled Baptiste out. They put me in there so there would be a better synergy between QA and AppDev. Apparently Baptiste had been telling them that the deployment issues had something to do with the quality of the applications. What a lot of dross. But they gave me both groups and when I was in charge they worked well together."

I'd always thought of QA as a semi-independent activity … like internal audit. Their job was to be a fresh set of eyes making sure that all was up to the requirements of the activity taking place. QA verified that use cases were developed by AppDev based on requirements, then tested by the business to ensure conformity to those requirements.

"That's something new to me," I offered. "I'm unaccustomed to seeing companies where those two teams report to the same person."

"Maybe you need to get out more often," offered Vlad with a snorting laugh. "I think it is the wave of the future. People are too constricted in their thinking … wanting every organization to be independent. That just leads to a lot of isolated and uncommunicative towers."

Vlad leaned across his desk. "Everybody in every company reports to the CEO. As you go up the organization all the groups work for the same people. Thinking QA and AppDev should report to different people is just not looking at the big picture. Successful application delivery is much more than just meeting the requirements. The world changes quickly. You need to integrate and deliver quickly, too. That means you need fast feedback and improvement loops and you can only get that if everyone in the solution lifecycle is working in sync … together. You can't just go off in a corner and build something and present it for quality checks when the whole thing is done. The tighter aligned everyone is for the entire lifecycle, the better the result. I'm sure that's why they put me in charge of both. And I have a certificate to show I'm trained in QA."

Vlad pointed to a slightly faded certificate on the wall. I couldn't see the date, but it must have been some time ago.

"But some geek in audit started talking just like you and they took QA away from me and gave it to this new victim … Ratana. But she seems to have a hook into it since they haven't fired her yet. Ratana and I are tight. We go rock climbing every couple of weeks. She's a certified lead climber. I'm still back with the top rope newbs, but I will get there. Everybody has to learn from the beginning. But we spend enough time together that if there is an issue developing we can work it out before it becomes an issue."

He continued, "The biggest problem revolves around the egos and goals of the top leaders. This whole release issue has been going on for years. We've tried several times to fix it. People like yourself came in to provide us with a solution, but got the boot when their answer didn't help. Problem is no one in leadership wants to talk about those times. If you're a senior leader it is really important not to let the troops see you bleed, cause if you can goof up and make mistakes, then people start to wonder how you are better than they are ... why you get paid so much more than they do ... why you get to tell people what to do. So once a leader is shown to be mortal, the other leaders tend to force them out. Partially because they see it as weakness, but more importantly, so the average employee won't see it and wonder if the other leaders are weak too. That's why they grab at any solution that might fix it and punish those who are offered it if it later proves not to be the answer."

"I understand your confusion," said Vlad. "Think of all the ways AppDev can mess up a release."

He began counting them off on his fingers. "We can do the right thing wrong by building a product that meets the customer requirements but our work is defective. Worse, we can do the wrong thing right by building something that works perfectly but doesn't meet the business requirements. We can build something that works well and meets the stated customer requirements, but does not produce the solution they need and desire. We can build what the customer asks for, what they need to solve their problem, and that works well, but it takes so long that by the time we finish, the original requirements are obsolete."

Vlad slapped his hands down on the top of his desk. "And those are just some of the ways we can blow it when building it. Beyond that there are other ways we can fail. We can hose it up by producing operational instructions on how to use the app that are unintelligible to anyone outside those who helped develop it. Or we can do a miserable job training people on the new application. We can fail to develop a back-out plan that would actually result in no net impact to the business should a problem arise. And that doesn't even start to include all the ways QA can cause deployment to fail. Given all the ways to fall down, I consider it a huge achievement that anything actually gets deployed, much less really works."

"I always thought of those as being part of a lifecycle," I said. "And that AppDev has a part in it, but so do other groups. That's one of the reasons QA is there. They help test it all to make sure the parts go together."

"Sorta right," said Vlad. "AppDev knows where the danger zones are. So we know where to make double sure it is working okay before we move it forward. And while QA owns testing to collect data on known defects, we let them know where to work so that we can work together to do a kind of proactive problem management before the solution is released. Only an idiot enjoys doing the same coding twice. And we are not idiots. That's why we're updating Asgard based on any and all issues from the initial release."

"That sounds right to me," said Zak. "Your team can get ahead of the curve by getting started on things now. But if, when we talk to other teams, we find something that needs to be adjusted, can we count on your support to make additional changes and help to get them in place for the next release"?

Vlad cocked his head and stared at us for a moment. "Sure. I guess so. Although I'll be amazed if you can find anything we haven't already started working on. I firmly believe that people are trying to get to that elusive sixth sigma cause, that's what's in the books. But books aren't reality. No one gets to perfection. No one deploys apps without issues occasionally cropping up. The problem is, our senior leadership has been reading … no," he chuckled. "Given some of the things they have said and done, I'm not sure they can even read."

"Seriously," he said. "The problem is that those leaders have been exposed to some theoretical information that describes how things work in a classroom and not the real world. So they have expectations more in line with concepts than with reality. Until they get their heads straight, they are never going to be happy with the results, no matter who produces them. Don't let them push you around just because they are your boss. Stand up for your individuality."

I was thinking about how that was easy for Vlad to say, but when you were on the other end of the organizational pyramid, things looked a little different, when Zak piped up and said, "Thanks for your support and insights. We really appreciate it."

I stared at my lap and shook my head. Zak could flip from being an insightful pro to a useless piece of baggage in a heartbeat, without any warning. There was no consistency. He was maddening. But maybe he was inadvertently pointing out something I'd never realized until now. Not everything improved or grew at the same rate, and it was our job to put this in sync.

Knowledge that would have helped Chris

- There are a number of ways application development may cause or contribute to a release deployment failure. At a minimum, it is important to check all of these risk points for each item in a release, as well as the connection points between inputs from other areas and outputs further downstream. Until you can verify the integrity at each of these risk points, do not let the release proceed.

- Don't be fooled into thinking that only one process can fail at a time. AppDev can simply build something that does not meet the specified requirements, or even does not work at all. This should never get past use case testing by the QA organization, but it has happened. In that case, there were multiple process areas that failed together.

- Communication and training by the AppDev team, regarding the changes in the new release, can also contribute to failure. If the support documentation in the form of run books, service desk work notes, user training or support documentation is deficient, there can be a failure of the release.

- If insufficient planning took place in developing the deployment back out plans, you could end up in a state where a defective release has been pushed into production but there is no effective way to back it out, and the only way to remedy the situation is to fix it in live production without impacting other applications.

CHAPTER 8: INFRASTRUCTURE – PHYSICAL CLOUDS

Zak and I were sitting in Pat's office, waiting for her to arrive. She'd sent a text saying she was running late, but that we should just go into her office and sit down. I always felt uncomfortable sitting in someone's office without them there – even with their direction to do so. It was kind of like walking into someone's home when they weren't there, making myself a snack and watching a movie. It always felt like a violation of their space.

Zak was sitting beside me with his eyes closed, his earbuds in and the music loud enough that I could almost sing along. But maybe it wasn't really that loud. Maybe his entire head was hollow and simply formed a resonating chamber that passively amplified the sound.

I was always amazed at how much people's offices were so different. Perhaps their workspace was simply an external simulation of what it was like inside their head … how it was a reflection of how they viewed the world. If that were true in Pat's case, I had to wonder how she could even think.

The room lighting was off, with the blinds down and nearly closed tight across her windows, as if sunlight were so deadly it would cause her to disintegrate into a pile of ashes at its first touch.

Pat's office looked like file drawers full of paper had exploded and scattered their contents into piles all around the room. Books and old-fashioned three ring binders were stacked horizontally in piles on the shelves of her bookcase. Even the pictures on her wall were hanging askew.

Apparently even Zak noticed it. "I haven't seen so much paper in one place in my entire life," laughed Zak. "Talk about a museum exhibit … hasn't she heard about electronic files? What would she do if she needed something and she was in another building? What if she switched devices? She'd have to copy everything over to the new device. I mean, how can she even find anything here? Where is her index? What's the taxonomy of her data? This looks like the Cloud after a heavy thunderstorm."

He reached onto her desk and pulled a small stack of papers from the top. He fanned them in his hands and then held them up to his nose. "They even stink from all the people that have been handling them," he said.

"Put that back," I snapped. "Do you walk into other people's homes and begin picking things up and pawing through them"?

Zak nodded. "Sure. Don't you? How else are you going to know anything about them"?

I made a mental note to never invite Zak to my house and said, "Just put it back now. What if she walks in and sees you digging through her private information? Do we really need anything else adding to the negative attitudes we've been seeing"?

Zak dropped the papers onto Pat's desk. They made a loud plop and threatened to spill across the other piles … potentially creating an avalanche sliding off the desk and on to the floor. He immediately stood up and began walking around the room. He bent down and looked under Pat's desk.

"What are you doing"?

"I've never met Pat," he said, as he continued inspecting her office. "But by the look ..." he wrinkled up his nose. "And what will probably be the smell, Pat's got to be as much an antique as the way she stores her data. I expect to find some punched cards and PROM chips laying around here somewhere ... not to mention pieces of moldy pizza and rancid coffee. Why is she working in IT"?

I'd never seen someone who was supposed to be a leader act like such a little child. I could not figure out what Megan saw in him. All I knew was that I did not want to get the same reputation he must have with people outside IT.

"Please get over here and sit down," I pleaded. "I've got to assume that Pat's working in IT because she is very good at what she does and the people she works for value that more than how she arranges her office. If it works for her and lets her get her work done, who are we to challenge that"?

Zak threw himself down into the chair beside me with a grunt, an instant before Pat walked in through the door.

I was a little taken aback. Pat looked like she should still be in school and was barely old enough to have a driver's license, yet here she was, a director in IT. It was not the image I was accustomed to seeing. Usually directors showed the wear and tear of years of service, but Pat looked more like an intern.

Pat was quite petite, wearing denim with dirty knees and a yellow company shirt celebrating the launch of our CSM product last year. The shirt was streaked with dust and dirt, as were her hands and forearms. Her blond hair hung down her back between her shoulder blades in a hastily tied long braid, giving it the appearance of a devolved queue. A tattoo of the thorny stem of a rose was barely visible peeking out from under her right sleeve.

She had that relaxed spring in her walk and moved the way highly conditioned athletes move … the kind of gait that radiates potential energy … just like a coiled spring. I half expected her to parkour off the wall, cat leap her bookshelf, kong vault over her desk and slowly drop into her chair as if she were in zero-g. I was slightly disappointed when she just walked past us, spun her chair around and threw herself down with a grunt.

With no introductions or preamble, she stared straight at us and said, "Why did you want to speak to me"?

"Hi Pat, we haven't met before. My name is Zak and this is my associate, Chris." He reached across the desk to shake her hand, but she extended her fist instead.

"Sorry, don't shake hands. Just spreads disease."

Zak shrugged and bounced his fist against hers.

"Look," she said. "Now that we have the pleasantries out of the way, can we get down to the subject at hand"?

"In a hurry for your next meeting"? asked Zak. "I'd rather have burning pencils shoved into me than sit through all those presentation marathons you must have to do."

Pat tried unsuccessfully to stifle a laugh with her hand and instead produced a loud snort.

"That's why I don't sit through presentations. Before this meeting I was in the data center crawling underneath the raised floor trying to locate dead whips to be pulled out so we'd have space to route new machine to machine connections. Because my predecessor was such a lazy slob, they just laid new ones as they needed but never pruned and recycled the dead ones. And that is where I am going once we finish here. So let's get this over."

"You were crawling underneath the floor"? asked Zak, before I could speak. "But you're a director. Why didn't you send one of your workers to do it? That's a nasty, dirty job."

Pat stretched out her shirt, looked at the dirt smears and with mock surprise said, "You think so? You think I might get my clothes dirty? Gee, I never thought of that. Guess I should have worn something I didn't care if it got dirty, unlike this shirt some idiot in marketing passed out to celebrate the release into production of a poorly designed and even more poorly built lump of software, which was so defective when implemented that my team was working round the clock for days just to convince the fools in AppDcv that it wasn't a hardware problem ... that it was their junk code. That's why this shirt is my favorite and why I cherish it above all my other clothes."

Zak started to laugh, but Pat cut him off. "Don't laugh. It's not funny. I have no patience for idiots who waste my time or the time of my team members. Do not underestimate me or my team. I am a polymath with an IQ of 185 who earned master's degrees in mathematics and physics by the time I was 16 and because I was too young to get a job, spent the time until I was 18 getting a doctoral degree and doing post-doc work in computer science and numerical theory. I crawl under the floor because I am physically smaller than anyone else on my team. The idiot building designer called for a floor raised only 12 inches and I doubt that designer would fit without getting stuck or ripping out more cable ... most likely because of results from their excessive daily beer consumption. So I get to play gopher. Great use of my time."

"Ah, you mean instead of having six-packs, they all had kegs"? giggled Zak.

"Not funny and trite. Titles are what go on business cards. The smartest person in the room should be in charge and while I am still ignorant of many things, that is often me. Same holds true of physical tasks. Like they say, 'Get the right tool for the job.' And in this case I am the right tool and I get the job done. That's the same thing I demand of every member of my team, or else they get moved to a new team."

"But why even mess with the hardware"? I asked. "We use private and hybrid Clouds at this company. Why don't we just get rid of all that hardware junk"?

Pat rolled her eyes and then turned to Zak, "Is he kidding me? I sure hope he doesn't work for you."

Pat wagged her finger at me and said, "This may come as a shock to you, but since the Cloud stuff started there are even more servers and devices in data centers now than there used to be."

I started to respond, "But that's not ..."

Pat cut me off. "What do you think the Cloud really is? Do you really think it means abandoning all the hardware in the world because computing now takes place through the magic of phlogiston with no need for corporeal manifestation of any kind? Cause if you do, be prepared for a shock. I have actually placed my hands on bare metal hardware running apps whose users are going to the Cloud, as recently as this morning. The Cloud just means you can get to things from anywhere, using any kind of device. It's the precursor to enabling the Internet of Things. But other than that, someone, somewhere, has to manage the machines that make it all happen. That so-called Cloud is only how it seems from the user perspective. For the rest of us IT trolls, not much changes."

"That doesn't seem right to me," I said.

"I'm not here to waste my time debating with you how many virtual servers can fit on the head of a pin, or any other metaphysical time sinks. At the request of my boss, I agreed to burn a hole in my calendar because you needed my help. If this is all you want, we are done."

"I've got this," said Zak to me. He smiled at Pat and said, "We are the owners of release and implementation ..."

"No, you are not," said Pat. "You may own release, but you're definitely not implementation. Otherwise it would be you trying to wriggle under the floor tiles in the data center."

"Hmmm ..." said Zak, with a look that I interpreted as him wondering if that would be fun and worth a try.

"Of course," I said. "Could you please share with us what you see in the release process that supports or hinders your team in its deployment efforts? What could we do better that would reduce the burden on your team"?

"Implementation is near the end of the lifecycle leading up to making an app live in production," said Pat. "We need a properly designed ... properly tested ... fully functional application. We need it so that we aren't the default when people start to point fingers during failure. Since everyone seems to have been seduced by this idea of a magical Cloud that somehow provides instrumentality without any physicality, my team is viewed as an anachronism from the days of magnetic tape and punched cards, so we must be the source of the issue. After all, magical goodness like the all-powerful, all-seeing, all-knowing cloudsphere is much too modern to be associated with any defects. So every time you mess up a release, my team has to waste valuable time proving it wasn't us. We are considered guilty until we can convince people otherwise.

Take that mess, Asgard. I can't speak to the design or build, but there was no way it could have been tested. Tested apps don't start throwing errors and try to take down the entire server the moment they are stood up. I don't know how they managed to build it that way, but in addition to corrupting data everywhere, they destroyed the virtual server and even somehow managed to crash the physical server it was running on. That takes real coding skill … or incompetence. Sometimes there is very little difference."

"But it was tested," protested Zak. "Vlad and the QA team tested it as much as they were able to …"

"Have you met Vlad"? asked Pat. After a rather long pause to let her comment sink in, she added, "That should be your answer right there."

Zak said, "He did the best he could. Our system environment is not segregated in any way. It's big, flat and open. It grew that way organically for years when it was all physical, and to make things easier, the physical environment was simply replicated as our core Cloud. That meant less retraining for our developers and allowed them to build things faster, although that unfortunately meant bringing over all of the modifications that had been made when it was completely physical. But I remember the discussions prior to that decision and how leadership decided it was worth the cost savings and speed of migration. They were told that our Clouds would be flexible enough to work around those weaknesses."

Pat shook her head in seeming disbelief. "So you're telling me that if someone hacks past our edge security and gets in, then they will have free run of the entire environment? Do you enjoy having our customer records shared with everyone on the web or held for ransom"?

"Our security is tight," said Zak. "At least that is what our experts tell me. It's their area of accountability. You're not responsible if they are wrong, so don't worry about it. People need to focus on how to make their own areas better, not critiquing those owned by others."

Pat rolled her eyes. "If you say so. But that still doesn't answer why apps come to us that are unstable."

Knowledge that would have helped Chris

- Unfortunately a lot of IT's business partners have a mistaken understanding of what Cloud technology is and what it can do. Too many of them take the metaphor too literally. The need for physical infrastructure continues to grow rapidly, even just to support virtual environments. The challenge is that often senior leadership, especially on the business side of the house, will read popular articles referring to Clouds and virtual technology and be misled about what is required to provide that functionality. They confuse the experience from the user side with the capabilities necessary in IT to provide it.

- However, one of the great impacts of virtualization is greatly increased platform stability. It's not unbreakable, but through reliance on virtual systems, the average impact can be reduced to seconds per year. These systems can fail during a deployment and people are still required to maintain the underlying infrastructure. Additionally, there will be times when there needs to be releases of this supporting infrastructure to support the virtual production environment. It can be subject to the same risks as any other release in terms of requirements, design, testing and deployment. The wise choice is not to forget about it when providing the business with a Cloud based experience.

CHAPTER 9: QA – GUARDIANS OF THE GATES

It had taken us a long time to arrange the meeting with Ratana. She was heavily booked, due to some project her team was focused on. That left us with less time to analyze the data and prepare recommendations for the senior leaders. But at least we finally got the slot and now it was here.

Ratana was rearranging the documents on her desk when we arrived. It didn't appear that anything was actually being added or removed. She seemed to just be moving them a couple of centimeters one way and a moment later moving them back. It wasn't clear to me if she was bored, being precise, or suffered from some sort of obsessive compulsive disorder.

Ratana was a small woman, slightly built, but well dressed in a crisp, professional dark suit that seemed to shift between black and dark blue depending on how the light struck it. A pale pastel silk scarf was tied around her neck that perfectly matched her crisp fresh blouse. Although she wore very little jewelry, the watch and simple strand around her neck looked high quality and very expensive. While she wasn't a minimalist like Juan from sales and marketing, her look was focused on a few items of high quality, rather than a multitude of inexpensive bright and shiny objects.

As we sat down, I noticed the sounds of Mozart's Für Elise playing in the background. Barely audible, the more I concentrated on them, the more they seemed to fill the entire volume of the room with their pastel tones … calming my mind and opening up a flow of creativity. It was like her personal look … a small set of instruments producing something of amazing quality, rather than an entire orchestra overwhelming all other thoughts with bombast and pyrotechnics.

Ratana had none of the professional certificates or photographs on her walls as most of the leaders in the company seemed to favor. Instead, she had decorated the space with a carefully curated personal exposition of travel and family photographs. There were comfortable shots of smiling adults and children in various locations. Many of them tropical. Beautiful shots of sites around the globe occupied a large section of the display, many from the towering heights of cliffs that were overwhelming enough to bring on vertigo.

Zak walked up close to the photographs and studied them intently. "These nature photos are really amazing, Ratana. You ought to consider putting them together with some kind of travelogue in a book … you know, something that adds even more color to the image and truly immerses people … gives them a tiny taste of the pleasure you had by being there."

"Zak," she said. "As usual, you are overly kind. But I take pictures for my own enjoyment and to document events in my life. They're just my futile attempt to hold on to each moment in time a little longer."

"They are very beautiful," I added. "We want to respect your hold on each moment by making the most of the time you have set aside for us. As you may know, the Asgard release did not do as well as expected in the live production environment."

Ratana nodded.

"And as you might imagine, as Zak and I try to identify what improvements can be made, we're seeing a lot of accusatory finger pointing. No one wants their team to be spotlighted to leadership as the responsible group."

"And because of our role, everyone immediately thought of the QA and testing team," said Ratana.

"Well, your group is responsible for ensuring that all is right with the app before it is approved for production. And I assume your team did sign off on Asgard"? I responded.

Ratana nodded. "Asgard was the largest release my team evaluated since I took it over from Vlad. We'd done a number of small items with no real issue and I was happy with our new direction up to that point. With Asgard being such an important release, my team applied maximum effort to testing and verification to ensure all would go well. While I was quite upset there were faults in the release, after reviewing the history of releases that passed through QA under Vlad and their frequent failures, I didn't feel quite as bad. Vlad is an amazing person and a wonderful friend, but his leadership record was such that there was … shall we say, significant room for improvement"?

Zak laughed, but I ignored him. He was a leader, yet he was worse than a two year old child. The more I worked with him, the angrier I got that I had to constantly cover for him.

"Evaluating other releases is not within the scope of our mandate to evaluate," I said. "While you are not the first leader we have visited, I think anyone would put your team early in the discussion, regardless of the history. And understanding the history, I think leadership would expect some rapid and material improvement from this team under your leadership."

"Hang on a minute, Chris," said Zak. "I think you may be getting ahead of yourself here. I've worked with Ratana for years and regardless of the area, her teams always produce quality deliverables. Whether development, training, or any other area, they have always done a great job under her leadership. But you seem to be implying that her team failed, even though we have no information supporting that."

I resisted the urge to point out that the app was approved and signed off by Ratana as being fully tested to the company's quality standards. Once they had signed off on it, the only way for it to go bad would be for someone further downstream, during the install or actual operation, to not only fail in their work, but to do such a terrible job that it completely degraded the app and caused it to fail. But given the next stop after QA was implementation, if the app had been good when Ratana passed it on, the only other team that could have impacted it would have been Pat's.

"I did not intend to imply anything. I'm merely trying to gather information. That's what Zak and I are both trying to do."

I turned to Ratana. "Perhaps you would like to share with us any insight you have as to what happened to Asgard? You must have some idea of what happened and how we can all improve"?

"QA is subject to every good or bad decision that happened before it gets to us," she said. "If the requirements are weak or don't point to a solution that meets the customer's needs, it can become a failure, even though everything turns out right from a QA standpoint. In other words, the entire IT organization has built the wrong thing right, so no matter how consistent it performs with what we believe requirements to be, it will still fail from our customer's standpoint," said Ratana. "So it is very possible that we could test and approve an app that because of failures in the requirements or changing business need, is no longer useful and may even be harmful. Likewise, if the use cases are incomplete, the training is totally inappropriate to the constituency and we will have problems."

"But the customer signs off on those requirements," I said. "So that should never be a problem. They sign off on them and as long as we build to that and confirm that we've built it, this is nothing more than an academic hypothetical."

"One would hope so," said Ratana. "Unfortunately, that is not how the customers always look at it. You should be on the receiving end of some of their calls after we build to and deploy the solution they specified."

"Been there. Got the t-shirt and it didn't fit. Still don't want to go back for another one," said Zak.

"That's okay, Zak. Your concern is appreciated," said Ratana. "Vlad and his team have been updating the app based on the results and feedback we've had from the initial release of Asgard. He seemed quite confident that his team had caught everything. We're going through the entire Asgard app right now, running all of the tests and doing a thorough quality check in preparation for imminent re-launch of Asgard or as we now call it, Asgard v2.0."

"Whoa," said Zak. "You must be eager for the haters from the business to get up in your face."

I asked Ratana, "Do you think you should wait moving forward with that until we review our findings with senior leadership and review the direction on how to move forward? We haven't yet identified the issues behind the original failure of the Asgard rollout, much less presented any recommendations to senior leadership. We are going to do the same thing all over again and somehow expect to be successful this time. Don't you think leadership would like to make this call"?

"Leadership is way ahead of you," she said. "That's why they are in leadership. They reached out to me and directed me to move forward. I raised the same issues you just did, but with the work that Vlad's told them his team has accomplished, they feel the benefits of Asgard working far outweigh the risks. They directed me to execute and prepare for implementation as quickly as possible. And that is what my team has done."

Ratana folded her hands together on her desk and said, "Think of it this way. Moving forward based on direction from senior leadership just cleared what were now a whole bunch of pointless meetings from your calendar."

Vlad never told us he was that far along. I had gone away with the assumption he was just starting … performing some proactive work to get hold of what would undoubtedly be a tight timeline once the decision was made to move forward.

This was madness.

Knowledge that would have helped Chris

- There are a number of ways quality assurance may cause or contribute to a release deployment failure. They have the role of overseeing one of the final checkpoints to ensure that the release can be deployed, without impacting the existing environment in a negative way. When they sign off on the release there should be a very high level of confidence it will be successful. Until they can affirm that, you should not proceed with the deployment.

- QA and AppDev generally don't fail together. That's because QA performs almost an audit like role on the work of AppDev, ensuring that it was done to the specification of the requirements. That doesn't mean you shouldn't check the flows into and out of QA. About the only time you will see them fail together is if AppDev produces release products that do not meet the requirements and QA's verification is either weak or broken and it misses it. When that happens, the results can be catastrophic. Always assume the worst and hope for the best.

- QA testing can sabotage the deployment if they fail to articulate and track the known errors they identify, or if they overstate how much under control the known error is. Evaluate known errors very carefully to ensure you are confident you have identified the true root cause and that the associated workaround will be successful for all scenarios the application will reasonably be expected to encounter. You should also ensure that if you plan to remediate the known error, that the timeline and resources required are appropriate to do so before the release is signed off.

- QA can inadvertently create a potential failure scenario if they consider the release static and in isolation. If an app is expected to grow in production, requiring more resources, storage, processing power, etc., and QA does not consider that dynamic, it may approve deployment of an app that will outgrow its environment and create issues.
- QA activities need to be structured to align tightly with the development approach they control. This applies to both psychological and procedural elements.

CHAPTER 10: MANAGEMENT INTERVENTION

We were walking faster than I had ever seen Zak move. He wasn't the plodder type, it just always seemed that he somehow knew that things wouldn't really get going until after he got there. The maddening part was that for the most part so far, he seemed to be right. And it was really beginning to tick me off. If I were late to a meeting … even by ten minutes, I would usually miss the first part and get chewed out for it afterwards. But Zak would stroll in, make some self-deprecating remark and give a pat on the back to some friends and then everything would start over again. I guess longevity and relationships made a much larger difference here than I had given them credit.

That's why I was confused. For the first time, Zak seemed to be a little bit concerned, or maybe even worried, that Megan had accelerated the re-launch of Asgard so quickly after the debacle of the first launch. I could understand the concern. We owned the release process and we didn't even know what the issue was yet. It didn't make any sense. It was basic IT support 101. If you had an issue and you don't know why you had the issue, what the root cause was, what it took to fix it, or if you had it remediated … then you were a fool to do it again and expect different results. It meant that we were likely to get slammed when it failed. The only question that would remain unanswered was who would be the one thrown under the bus.

The one upside I could see at the moment was that Zak was relatively silent, maybe for the first time in his life.

"What do you think Megan had in mind when she okayed this"? I asked, hoping to see if Zak had any bits that I didn't. After all, he had been here a lot longer and seemed to know the nuances of everyone quite well. "I just can't believe she did it."

Zak picked up the pace.

I pestered him again. "We just need to find out and get the rest of the facts. Asgard needs to go back through a full cycle. We need to reconfirm the details of each use case from the users ... not to mention the reconfirmation of critical success factors and business requirements and then a recycle of use case testing and verification. There's a month's worth of work just to understand why it failed. Doesn't she understand that? Doesn't she realize that if ... or maybe when, it fails again next week, she will get slammed for it, as much as I guess you and I will"?

I couldn't believe I had just said that. Here I was, still new enough on the job that I had to think twice on how to find my cube, and already I was being set up to get wacked because a group of senior leaders were determined to push out a flawed release.

"I don't know. I just don't know."

I had never heard Zak use that phrase before. Maybe he was on a performance plan and with one more failure he was out and then I would be what I was supposed to be ... in charge. For an instant, there was part of me that wondered if I should help him tumble over the edge. Maybe that was why I was here. After all, it was not the kind of thing Megan would say directly to me – a recent new hire, about a long term employee. It would be more of a, "nudge – nudge – wink – wink" thing. Maybe I was the change agent and by hiring me to do it, Megan made it easier on herself to move Zak out.

10: Management Intervention

It wouldn't be the first time a leader had put someone on a performance plan that was impossible to achieve, with no thought of rehabilitation. I'd already been threatened with it. Zak had some interesting professional skills and was an okay human being, but did I want the job I'd joined this company for badly enough to help push him out the door and take a smaller, but not job killing rebuke ... hopefully to the unsaid gratitude of Megan. I wasn't sure. The more I thought about it, the more sense it made, but the more it felt the wrong thing to do to him.

Zak came to a quick halt, not too far from my cube.

"Wait in your cube. I want to have this conversation with Megan one on one," he said.

"No," I said. "I need to be part of this. You could use my help, if for no other reason than to add some more outside perspective."

Zak shook his head. "Sorry, but she will be much more candid if it is just one on one. Besides, you're the newbie here. You're not a complete tool, so if the re-release of Asgard 2.0 totally augers there will be some separation between you and it. Starting a new job bearing the weight of a disaster is no way to begin."

Zak pointed toward my cube. "Just go hang. I'll be back in less than an hour and will give you the full readout then."

Without waiting for my response, Zak turned and headed toward Megan's office. As he turned left at the next cross row, he glanced back to make sure I wasn't following him, like some lost puppy.

I stood there in the corridor, shaking my head, as people walked silently by. I couldn't believe it. Self-absorbed, unfocused and technically clueless Zak seemed to be doing something that benefited someone besides himself – me. How could I throw him under the bus now, even if it would get me the situation I had signed up for when I came here?

I slowly walked to my cube trying to reconcile everything in my head. How could someone as self-centered as Zak do something that appeared so selfless? It was only as I sat down that the thought occurred to me. What if he wasn't being selfless? What if he was lying to me? What if he was meeting with Megan by himself so he could toss me under the bus and save himself?

It was less than an hour later when Zak came walking down the aisle to my cube, bouncing along in his usual kinetic fashion.

I didn't wait for him to sit down before blurting out, "So what happened. Did she really approve something this week"?

Zak nodded his head. "She didn't have any choice. Juan of sales and marketing got the CEO and some of her peers to insist she make it happen. They don't understand what's involved."

"Why didn't she call on us"? I said. "We could have pitched them the whole release – deploy lifecycle ... gave them the perspective they need to make a more informed decision."

Zak shook his head. "She wasn't real specific, but I think they don't really want to know or even care. How we do it doesn't matter to them. They just looked at the amount of time since they originally asked for it and decided it had been long enough. If IT can't get it done in the timeframe they need it then they will consider other alternatives to having our IT do it. Doesn't matter to them who does it, as long as it gets done. We're talking about features and they want benefits."

As soon as Zak left, I headed to Megan's office. I knew that she was tightly scheduled and had a high probability of not being there, but if she were there it would be harder to ignore me if I were there in person.

I was slightly surprised when not only was Megan in her office with the door open doing paperwork, but that when she looked up and saw me, she waved from behind her desk. I wasn't about to let this opportunity go to waste. I marched in, closed the door and sat down across the desk from her.

She looked up and in a rather surprised voice said, "Is there something you need"?

"Yes, there is." Megan continued working on her documents even as I spoke, but I continued. "Your role gives you a much broader vision that I am not privy to, so with all respect, why are you forcing the re-release of Asgard this weekend, even though we barely understand what happened, much less why and how to fix it"?

Megan remained focused on her work and did not look up as she spoke. "Did Zak speak with you"?

"Yes, he did, but there were questions he could not answer."

"What specifically were those"? she asked and continued writing, her focus evidently elsewhere.

"The biggest one is understanding why you didn't let us help you explain the whole release – deploy lifecycle to leadership. Then they would understand all the things we need to do. Why can't we be allowed to give them all the information they need to make an informed course of action? Why are you holding us back"?

Megan looked up and slowly shook her head. "Zak didn't explain that"? She picked up a small, worn, bound notebook and wrote in it while looking directly at me.

"He explained it. It sounded like your words. But I don't think he understood a word of it. Zak is a really nice person, and he has interpersonal gifts that I envy. But I am not convinced he really understands what we are doing or what it takes to have successful deployment without disrupting the business. The process has been dysfunctional for so long, people are starting to see that as normal."

Megan made notes in her notebook all the time I was speaking, but she said nothing.

"I am just amazed that our company's leaders are making decisions without the benefit of all the information they need. Aren't they asking for the information from you? Aren't they asking why you are not giving them that information? I just don't get it. They are smart people. If Asgard was that big a fail, why aren't they insisting we produce some kind of 'after-action' response, identifying what to avoid going forward? Don't they want the read-out on that, even if for nothing better than finding someone to blame? I know that not all information is available when decisions get made, but I'm talking about critical information they could have for no more than the nod of their head. Doing the same thing again, so soon, makes no sense to me. It's like they are trying to make IT look bad so they can get rid of us and outsource the work."

10: Management Intervention

Megan sat back in her chair, took a slow, deep breath and began slowly tapping the fingertips of her hands together. "I can see why you are concerned and frustrated, Chris. But you're not really looking at this correctly. You're confusing features with benefits. All leadership wants to see are benefits. The 'how' doesn't really matter to them. That's an IT issue and it's up to us to figure out how to get them the benefits they need to execute the business strategy."

"But Asgard will fail this weekend, just like it did last weekend," I protested. "You hired me to fix and run the release and deployment activities here based on my experience. Well, I can tell you with great assurance that there is virtually no chance this weekend will be successful. Doing the same thing over and over and expecting something different each time, only works in games of chance, not deterministic activities like this."

"Failure is not a foregone conclusion," said Megan. "I've personally spoken to Ratana in QA. They have been very busy testing and overseeing adjustment to the app. Working with the AppDev team, they have identified a number of improvements and have managed to roll them into Asgard v2.0. I think you may be a little pessimistic – perhaps because there has been work going on that neither you nor Zak are part of, or perhaps because you have been so busy looking backward to track down root causes that you have missed the forward progress of our team. After all, IT is a team and we are all in this together. We've just been supporting you and Zak. You have a very difficult task and should be glad for all the help."

She paused for a moment and then added, "Actually, I'm a little surprised you never saw us working to help you. Perhaps you were very focused ..."

I interrupted her. "And when Asgard fails again this weekend ..."?

Megan cut me off. "You mean, if Asgard v2.0 fails ..."

I nodded, but everything I had learned and observed told me that the probability of success would be virtually nonexistent. If they had been doing anything with the amount of impact that was needed to fix Asgard, Zak or I would have noticed it. I started to wonder how much effort had actually been expended and how much of the results Megan had really conducted.

"Does that mean that if Asgard v2.0 fails, all of IT will share the displeasure of the business"?

"Of course not," snapped Megan. "Accountability rests with the release and deployment manager. It always has. They own the effectiveness of that lifecycle."

"So Zak is accountable"?

"No. That is the role we hired you for."

"But you told me things had changed between the time I accepted your job offer and the day I started ... that I was not directly working for you ... I was reporting to Zak. Isn't he the one who should be accountable"?

"Zak is the ITSM lead, but you are the release and deployment manager. Yes, you report to him, but you are also accountable for the success or failure of the deployment."

"What about change management? You can't release into production without an approved change request and the CAB has already met this week. This does not seem to be something that rises to the level of an emergency change."

"Actually, it does," said Megan. "And although I wouldn't expect you to know this so soon, since change management is not part of your area of responsibility, I can authorize an emergency change for any activity, at any time. However, in this case, I did not. There was no need to. Our change process does not require a CAB meeting. It only requires that the correct people sign off on the change. In this case, Bertha, our change manager, was happy to sign off. Since most of the adjustments we've made have been internal to the application, there really isn't much of a need to redo the request itself, other than to adjust for the new dates."

I couldn't believe it. I was being told they were going to throw me under the bus, but first they were going to blindfold me and tie my hands so I couldn't even see the bus coming. It seemed as though they had hired me simply to have a "new kid" that no one really knew, to become the sacrificial victim – the target of the company's displeasure at IT, without impacting any one of the current employees.

Megan spoke softly. "Chris, this may seem challenging to you and may even seem a little unfair, but that is not the case. You were brought on board to make this work. That is how I sold the idea of your req to my peers, because they had to give up one of theirs in order for me to hire you. One thing you need to understand about senior leadership is that they don't have the luxury of time. The business environment changes constantly and they have to react to it. So they expect everyone else to do the same. They do not have the time to give to support a solution that is pure and aligned by some conceptual academic concepts. They want results that yield benefits and they want them yesterday. And so you understand how real this is, I was already getting negative feedback about you … not just from the way you were interacting with leaders, but also that you seemed to be more focused on the theory than on the business issue of making this work now."

Megan sat back in her chair. She picked up her pen and used it to tap emphasis on the desktop as she spoke. "There was no choice. If we didn't re-launch Asgard, they were going to start questioning whether any of us should be here."

"So they don't care ...""?

Megan cut me off. "No, they care very much. They care about the company, their legacy and all of the people who make a living here. And just as important, they care about their compensation which is heavily slanted toward achieving near term results. And that is why you are going to be under intense scrutiny for Asgard v2.0. While you and I know that there has been little you could do under the circumstances, you must also know there will be deep and serious questions about your ability to perform this role if it fails."

"What does that mean? Is that a warning, a chastisement, a suggestion or what? And in plain language, please."

Megan shook her head. "If Asgard v2.0 doesn't work, they will expect you to be placed under some enhanced structured management guidance to remediate your ability to perform at the required level ... in other words a very harsh performance improvement plan from which there would be little chance of recovery. Is that direct enough for you"?

"Do you want me to talk to them directly"? I asked. "Perhaps because I have the most recent insight into how other companies are handling this type of situation. Maybe they will listen to me."

Megan shook her head and laughed. "Please tell me you are not that clueless and you said that only as a joke, because if you do that, they won't even bother with the formality of a performance plan. They will give you the boot before your meeting with them is over ... if you can even get any of them to meet with you. Their administrators have standing orders that nobody below them in the company can see them ... nobody, no how, no way. They are much too busy. You may speak with them only when summoned. And you have not been summoned."

No matter how much Zak looked like he'd changed and was standing up for the team, both he and Megan were only interested in one thing ... making sure they were not the ones crushed because senior leadership was more interested in activity than success. And all the while leading me to believe he was the one standing up, and if needed, taking one for the team. I was the newbie. I had less time in than they did, so I wasn't as valuable. I hadn't earned my protection yet.

From the back of my mind I began to think about what it would take to get someone else to end up under the bus beside myself. And I really wanted that person to be Zak.

Knowledge that would have helped Chris

- Most project plans are built right to left. That is, the first step is to establish when the deliverable is due and then work backwards from there. It is the fixed point from which everything else is determined. With a fixed delivery date, all of the activities necessary to achieve it must be manipulated and adjusted to meet it.
- It is not uncommon for leadership to pull the fixed delivery date in, closer to the present, without serious consideration of what needs to be done to make it happen. This is not due to bad intent on their part. They are reacting to the needs of the business and requiring IT to be as agile as the rest of the company must be in responding to market and competitive forces.

CHAPTER 11: CHANGE MANAGEMENT – SHORT CIRCUIT

I was waiting outside Bertha's office. I understood she was coming back from a change management meeting on the other side of the building. I'd sat through a couple of them and that was plenty for me. I had no desire to sit through another just to ensure I had her attention. But she was late and even though I had come here directly from Megan's office, and she had agreed to meet with me based on a hastily fingered text outside Megan's office, I was still irritated.

When I was an operational manager charged with meeting tight delivery deadlines, I'd never liked change management. They always seemed to appear out of nowhere at the worst possible time and add no value beyond making your life more difficult. I'd always thought of them as being the company's way of not so subtly saying, "We don't trust you to conduct enough due diligence to make sure your changes cause no harm to anyone else, so we're going to turn some hard case loose on you to inspect your work to make sure you know what you are doing. Oh and by the way, all this person will bring to the job is attitude. They don't know anything about the details of your craft."

"You Chris"? snapped an accusatory voice from behind me, in a tone that would have made the toughest drill instructor snap to attention. I shot a quick glance over my shoulder, but there was no one there.

A moment later, she came huffing and puffing around the corner, walking at a near trot, with huge piles of manila folders under each arm. Much to my surprise, she appeared to carry neither laptop nor tablet. I couldn't remember the last time I'd seen someone from IT who wasn't within arm's reach of one of those devices. She was wearing a dark blue pants suit that looked like it was a multi-generational hand me down from the last century. The pants seemed to have permanent wrinkles at the lap and the knees. Even her matching buttoned suit jacket looked like it had either spent the night wadded inside a suitcase or else she'd slept in it. Stains were visible on the dark blue scarf tied slightly too tight around her neck, adding to the flush of her face.

She halted for a moment to look me up and down, then jerked her head toward the door and said, "In the office." I felt like the first time I'd been sent to the principal's office. Before I opened my mouth I felt guilty … like I must have done something wrong, even if I were totally blameless. I wondered if she had to be trained to have this attitude or if she were born with it.

I'd heard she'd been the change manager for almost eight years and unless something strange happened, would be the change manager for at least another eight. You didn't see too many ex-change manager's moving up, or out, to provider roles. Not many people aspired to be career change managers. It was usually something one fell into, never to return. You had to have a certain view of the world to be good at it … not to mention a very thick skin and a willingness to be the bad guy on a regular basis – someone who understood that none of the pushback was personal, but that you were personally responsible for making sure changes were processed properly. You had to understand that people would not understand why you had to reject a change, regardless of how much sense it made. Bertha had a pretty thankless job that was also essential to the success of IT.

I was glad I had come here straight from Megan's office and left Zak to his own devices. I wanted to have this conversation by myself. If I were about to be sacrificed and tossed under the bus by the person who was now identified as my manager, I wanted to ensure I'd done everything I could to avoid being a helpless victim. And the first step was knowledge. You can't prevent what you don't know or understand. Once I had that, perhaps I could find an ally in Bertha.

Bertha's office was so neat and organized it would have made even someone with a pathological level of obsessive compulsive disorder feel claustrophobic and constrained. Strangely, she had three visitor chairs in her office, not the standard two most people at her level were assigned. There were a pair of them across the desk from her seat, but there was also one on the left side of her desk ... a little closer ... a little more direct.

She turned her back on me and began carefully putting her files into one of the tall four drawer cabinets against one wall. "Be with you in a minute," she said.

I started to sit down in the chair across the desk from hers. Without looking she snapped, "Not there," she said. "The chair beside the desk."

I sat down and a moment later she slid into her chair, slightly adjusted a few of the items on her desk ... lining them up, then pivoted her chair to me and in an annoyed voice said, "So you want to know where the fault is in our release process and what it means for Asgard v2.0? What makes you think I can tell you anything beyond what I've already contributed, especially since senior leadership has already spiked Asgard as an emergency exception"? Bertha punctuated her question by looking at her watch, before leaning over into my personal space. When I didn't immediately respond, she added an impatient, "Well"?

I was surprised at how intimidated I was by her voice, her tone and her actions. I understood now why she had me sit beside her desk instead of on the other side. It was much easier to assault my personal space that way. Intimidation was definitely her style. That must have been the way she maintained control over the various IT teams. I knew they could be a little caustic and apparently she countered that by being even harsher than they were.

"Well, your role in change gives you a unique perspective on the delivery of solutions," I said.

"Don't try to be a sycophant. I'm not responsible for the quality or efficacy of the solution. I certify neither its warranty nor its utility. I'm not a technical specialist and I doubt there is a person in the company who could do so for all aspects of a solution. The days of a geek in their mother's basement crafting a world changing application by themselves are long since gone … if they ever really existed."

I sat back in my chair and paused for a moment. Bertha wanted me to be intimidated. She wanted to be in charge and she wanted me to cede that to her … to acknowledge her ownership and control. If that were what it took to get what I needed from her, then that was what I would give her. I needed her help and if getting her help meant letting her be in charge on this, I was fine with that.

"I'm sorry, Bertha. I think I got off on the wrong foot here because I was so eager to hear your insights. I wasn't trying to insinuate that you were responsible for any issues that may have arisen as a result of the last release, or were the driver behind the forced Asgard v2.0 release. Far from that. It was because of your unique vision of the entire lifecycle that I thought you could see areas we should work on improving."

Her scowl relaxed a little. "I'll give you my observations, but if you continue being a kiss-up, the meeting is over. I see the best every CAB meeting and believe me, you are far from the best."

I chuckled quietly. "Fair."

"Understand the reality of change management," she said. "It's a check-box process. There are many tasks and deliverables associated with launching a new application that each functional area must complete. From the change process perspective, we check to see that all the steps are completed. We do not ..." She shook her finger at me. "And I want this to be abundantly clear. We do not verify that everything was done right. That's up to the subject matter experts for that area. All we do is get confirmation from them that it was done. We look at what they have identified that needs to be completed before launch, and then verify they have done that. And generally that verification is not done through anything we do. We again rely on the actions and assertions of other SMEs."

"So who is responsible for approving all the release if change isn't involved in that"?

"I never said change and release were not tightly linked," snapped Bertha.

"But you just said …"

"What I said," she interrupted, "was that release is just a highly specialized form of change and if you consider it from an academic perspective, every release does constitute a change to the production environment and will require approval of the CAB. And I assure you, that is not something I give out lightly. I need to see the CAB's collective approval on any release, as well as the sign-off of accountability from the leaders of each of the functional areas."

She began drawing a block image on a blank piece of paper. What amazed me was that she was drawing it upside down and right to left instead of left to right, so that it was easily readable for me, but totally backwards for her. I used to try to do that when explaining things to people, but it always came out an indecipherable mess, so I quit trying. Bertha, however, was producing a tight, accurate image that looked like it had been drawn in a normal position. And she was doing it just as fast as I could have done in a normal position. She was impressive.

Bertha poked one of the boxes at the start of the workflow. "We need solid requirements from the BAs on the business relationship team. We need a service level package that has been approved by the service portfolio manager. There has to be a service design package from the service design coordinator. Without that, no approval by the release manager …"

Bertha stopped and poked her right index finger at my face. "That's you, if you last … can be considered legitimate. Once you are satisfied everything is appropriate, you need to sign off on the release package and create a change request that is acceptable and complete to me. Only at that point does it get scheduled for the CAB and get reviewed like any other change. Releases should not be emergency changes and therefore it needs to queue up for the weekly CAB meetings. Once approved there, it still needs to be rolled into production and watched by the NOC and the service desk through 30 days of intensive care."

Bertha sat back in her chair. "That is a lot of work and it does not happen at a moment's notice."

"Are you saying I need to check in with everyone … all the subject matter experts in every discipline and get their input too? It'll take forever. What if the release of a new application is imminent"?

"Then you had best start early," she said. "Release is an entire lifecycle, not just deployment of a new app into production. As the release manager, you need to be involved as the overseer for each step. It is a very intricate lifecycle with a lot of moving parts. Making something complex sound simple means that you know how it works at a high level, not that you understand the nuances and corners in the process where things can easily get messed up. The proof of whether or not you truly understand something complex is if you can explain it quickly and simply."

She put her pen down and leaned over to me. "You're not just the person who opens the champagne at the end. You have to work for your money … just like I do."

I nodded. "The larger question I have … one that I would sincerely appreciate your guidance on … is a simple one, but with potentially extensive impacts." I had to test the waters with Bertha. If I were going to be able to build a coalition to halt this release before it did more damage, I would need her and a few others. The risk was that it could be viewed as being terminally insubordinate. But since it looked like I was the top candidate to get thrown under the bus when it failed, there wasn't a lot to lose.

I took a deep breath and said, "I have been told the plan is to re-release Asgard as soon as possible. Although business need is driving the urgency, based on my experience, I am concerned we, as a technical organization, are not as confident as we should be that the problem has been caught. I would like to understand your perspective on this."

"I think what you are evaluating is whether the impact to the organization is worse from releasing a defective product or by not releasing the defective product and hurting sales and revenue generation."

"That's a good way to put it," I said. "We have two unpleasant alternatives."

"In either case, the company suffers and revenue is reduced. And in the first case, the business views IT as producing junk, thus hurting revenue and in the second case, the business views IT as being unable to deliver anything of value, thus hurting revenue. I don't see much difference between the two. In either case, the business opinion of IT gets worse and revenue is impacted."

I nodded.

"And as you know," she said. "Senior leadership has already made their decision." She paused for a moment and then added, "I know you are aware of their guidance … and that you are not satisfied with it. But I think that is because you don't have a broad enough perspective. Can you say with certainty that Asgard v2.0 will not work as desired"?

I shook my head. "Of course not. I can't prove a negative like that. I just know that without …"

"To senior leadership it sounds like you are indecisive and looking for perfect and complete information before coming to a conclusion. They are quite comfortable working with imperfect partial knowledge. It is what they get paid for. Your failure to be able to work at that level swings their vote. Remember that from their perspective, IT is expendable. We are a capability and having us in-house is merely one way to deliver it. It is simple to blame us for whatever goes wrong and if too much goes wrong, they can always outsource the entire function."

"That hardly seems fair," I said.

Bertha laughed. "Fair has nothing to do with it. It is about the company's success and nothing more. That is why IT is here. If we are not giving the business what they need to make the company successful, then there is no reason to have us here."

"Is that why you signed off on the change associated with the re-release of Asgard v2.0 without a formal change review board meeting"?

Bertha's entire demeanor changed. She stood up and pointed to the door. "I intend to continue my current role at this company for some time. Our meeting is over."

I was still glad I hadn't brought Zak.

Knowledge that would have helped Chris

- The approval for deployment of a release is a specialized kind of change. In many companies the CAB does not do a detailed review of the contents of the release. Instead, they look for the approval of the release and deployment process owner. They will often focus on just the dates for deployment and the presence of back out plans.
- Typically the CAB will do this for reasons related to time and complexity of the contents of a typical release, and the impact of potentially holding back a critical business solution. While not totally unacceptable, this is a risky course from a change perspective. Not all constituencies in the CAB may have provided input or feedback on the release. It is very possible that there are issues they have which were never concerned during the design of the release.
- Too often the release and deployment process manager is focused on meeting challenging dates dictated by the business and a lower priority is placed on the other part of their responsibility ... ensuring that they are protecting the integrity of the environment during their actions. A good release and deployment process manager is as focused on change management as they are on increasing the capabilities of the business.

CHAPTER 12: RELEASE – LET SLIP THE DOGS OF WAR

Zak and I sat in the break room across from each other, but saying nothing. It was late on Friday. Most of the people in the building had left and gone home, excited about the upcoming weekend off. Unfortunately, we weren't among them. It had been a long frustrating day and even worse of a week. I wasn't sure if the quiet between us was due to nothing to say or if simply that we were both so beat we were past the point of being able to speak.

The first day here I'd brought in some of my favorite first flush Darjeeling tea. It was one of my guilty pleasures. It was an expensive indulgence and although I doubted this place could give me water at the temperature to properly brew it, I was so fried and stressed out that I wasn't sure I really cared. Zak was drinking a strange brew he called, "Tecoff Shots," or "Tecoff" for short. He'd taken a cup of coffee and cooked it in the microwave until it reached the superheating state. He then dropped a generic tea bag into it, which caused a flash to steam reaction, instantly brewing the tea in the coffee and extracting maximum caffeine and theobromine. To finish it off, he poured an energy shot into the steaming liquid. Zak offered one to me when he made his, but I declined based on the smell alone. It was probably the wisest thing I'd done all week, but it did help me understand where some of his seemingly boundless energy came from.

Zak took a couple more swigs from his cup and apparently the caffeine kicked in. "Tomorrow is the big overnight deployment of the new release."

He held his cup up in salute. "Asgard is dead. Long live Asgard v2.0."

I couldn't hold back my laugh. I just wish I'd gotten a video to post online. The gallows humor had set in a few days ago as I started working on my resume, since I knew I was going to get fired once this new release crashed and burned.

Swallowing a big gulp of Tecoff, Zak said, "You're set to be in the war room with the rest of us aren't you? I mean, I think … I hope that they picked up all the bugs. I know Ratana is having her team go through one final set of tests this afternoon. That's when we'll get to find out if they caught all the weirdness that hurt us before."

Zak slapped me on the shoulder. "Don't worry so much. I'm sure all the errors have been caught."

I nodded, but knew that even Zak didn't believe that. He was just trying to be … well, Zak. I had one last hope in my mind. The only way we can prevent a disaster is to quickly identify the cause of the issues with Asgard v2.0 and get it in front of leadership now … before the close of business today, by whatever means necessary. And if they fired me because of it, so what? They had set me up to get fired anyway, so why not get it done on my own terms, trying to save the company from its own delusions.

"Seriously," I said to Zak. "Let's go through this list one more time, just to make sure we've done all that we could do."

Zak gave a loud theatrical sigh. "You are taking this way to personally, but if it will get you to relax, fine. Go for it."

I tapped my tablet and my checklist popped up. "Thanks. Here's what I've got. Shallah of the BRM told us the requirements were right. So in her view that was not the source of the issue and there was nothing to change."

"Did she ever. I thought she was going to start beating you. Talk about stepped on toes and a short temper," said Zak. "I'm glad we don't have to spend any more time with her."

I shook my head, but said nothing. I knew what was wrong here, but nobody wanted to see it or hear it. Everything was locked in functional towers for each of the release lifecycle touch points. As long as each functional area thought their work was up to their standards, no one cared about the end to end process at all. That was the big mistake senior leadership was making. No one understood that this was a dynamic business environment where things were constantly changing, and that as a tool provider to the business, we had to be so agile we could adjust and deliver what was needed, when it was needed. But at this point, I was really getting sick of harping on that message over and over and over again.

"Let's keep going so we can tell Megan that either we have got everything covered or we have not," I said. "Asgard v2.0 is all that we are rolling out in this release, but we've still got assurances from Vlad that the whole release package is complete ... including a back-out plan if something goes wrong."

"Yep," said Zak as he slurped some more of his beverage. "We're really good at back-out plans."

I shook my head. "Being good at backing releases out because they have failed is not my idea of a skill we should advertise a lot. However, we've got everything new that has been done loaded into our ... dare I call a spreadsheet a, 'tracking system' so we can quickly spot the source of new errors."

Zak laughed and almost snorted out some of his Tecoff.

"Don't get too excited," I said. "I know going through this list is thrilling, but I don't want people to think I somehow killed you to get your job or something." Sure Zak was using me to protect himself, but I could not come up with a way to flip it around so he would take the hit like he should. With Megan on his side, I had no room to maneuver. The only road I could travel was to make it more difficult for him to pull the trigger because he thinks I am a nice guy, than to do it easily because I am nasty to him.

I kept going down the list. "Bertha never presented the release to the CAB for review and approval, but change request for the release was signed off by senior leadership so she had to accept it."

"I wonder if they read the change documentation and method of procedure like they are always yelling at us for not doing," smiled Zak.

"Enough," I said. My patience was wearing thin and I was finding it harder and harder to control my dislike for Zak. "We got confirmation that customers were all trained by Vlad's team on the original features of Asgard and on the changes that AppDev made, as well as making updates to the service desk run books so they can deal with any issues."

"Yeah, but Asgard is going to be on intensive care coverage for the next 60 days anyways, so whatever they get will be routed directly to the Asgard project team," said Zak. "And that's what we've got to analyze and report on for leadership. Don't worry, they will have a lot of support."

"Unless there are a lot of them," I said. "In which case, you'll be doing the reporting and I'll be walking out the door with a boot print in my rear end."

"Love the image," said Zak. "But let's hope it doesn't come to that."

The moment was pure Zak. He always found a way to make you like him, even when he was working you for his own benefit. Maybe he was in the wrong profession. Maybe he didn't belong to IT. Maybe he was full of raw sales potential at heart.

"Thanks," I said. "As far as I can think right now, we've covered most of the risks to a successful deployment. The run books in support and the service desk are up to date. QA has identified all the bugs spotted during the launch last weekend, and with the help of AppDev, hopefully squashed them."

Zak's phone vibrated and began playing some rave house music. He checked it and said, "And just in time. Megan is ready for our results. This should be fun."

A few minutes later we walked into Megan's office. She looked fresh and relaxed as if she had just come back from two weeks' vacation. If she were concerned about the upcoming deployment, she showed no sign of it. She was even smiling.

"So here are my problem solvers. Tell me, are you ready for the successful re-release of Asgard? Have you identified all the things that were wrong from last weekend and resolved them all"?

We sat down across the desk from her. Zak turned to me and said, "Why don't you start by telling Megan what we know."

"Okay. Actually, I'm going to touch on the areas where the original Asgard could have gone wrong first and then tell you who we checked with to ensure that everything has been addressed."

Megan leaned toward me and said quietly, "I'm glad you're with the program now." She leaned back in her chair and said to us, "You have my complete and undivided attention."

"Do you mind if I write on the whiteboard"? I asked.

Megan gestured toward it and nodded. "Please," she said.

The whiteboard was incredibly dirty. It looked as if no one ever cleaned it; they simply tried to smear the previous marks into a grayish patina spread across the entire surface. Flakes of dried marker ink dropped into the aluminum marker tray at the bottom of the board every time I tried to clean up some space for my chart. Someone had used the wrong type of markers before and despite best efforts, the faded ghosts of those diagrams and words would forever be part of that board.

I used a black marker to draw a grid on the board with three columns and about a dozen rows. At the top of the first column it said, "Team," atop the second column it said, "Issue" and on the last one it said, "Current Status".

I poked at the grid with the marker and said, "There are at least a dozen ways for an apparently solid release candidate to fail. A lot of them should be caught before or during deployment, but they do happen on a recurring basis. That's probably what has been going on here. That's why we started our assessment with the groups responsible for those areas. Think of these as areas where high performance by specific teams is needed - to ensure the delivery of the intended functionality matches the customer's requirements. These are the places where a small error can have immense consequences."

I snatched up a red marker, popped off the top and without thinking, indulged in one of my guilty pleasures. I sniffed the tip ... cherry. I had a non sequitur moment and wondered if anyone making these markers ever had a moment of frustrated rebellion and infused the ink with a scent that didn't match the color ... say a red marker that smelled like chocolate? Or if they were color blind, did they ever produce nothing but shades of alternate colors for cherry, lime or grape, yet retained those scents?

I reached down and took another sip of tea. "IT has functional domain towers of expertise in it. Try to think of the release and deployment process as a horizontal workflow that crosses each of these towers as it goes from initial requirements through to live production. How do we know if there are issues once the product goes into live production – things, such as, it doesn't work, doesn't work as expected, or is too difficult to use? Issues get raised by the business via the service desk, or even through direct contact with leadership."

Zak chuckled and Megan shot him a nasty look and snapped, "Zak." I smiled. At least I wasn't the only one who thought Zak was so very inappropriate at times.

Once Zak quieted down, I continued, "If the functionality of the new app turns out to be inappropriate for the needs of the business, then the issue, most likely, is rooted in

Shallah's BRM team, as they are responsible for providing the rest of the IT teams with the requirements and critical success factors. It means we did the wrong thing right. Shallah assures us that she is confident her team correctly translates what the business wants into what the business needs, in a way that IT can address, and that the requirements for Asgard v2.0 are identical to the ones they submitted for the original Asgard."

"Yes," added Megan. "I like the fact that she understands the importance of providing what the business needs. Buyers are liars as she always says."

I still hated that idea. It was too close to the old-school IT of us providing the business with what we thought they should have and hoping they would go away after that. But it seemed to be the way IT viewed their relationship here at this company and given the thin ice I was on, I saw no reason to push this right now. Perhaps later, if by some miracle I were still around, I'd start working on that.

I took a deep breath and moved on. "Yes, and as we investigate the source of the issue in an attempt to remediate it, there are a number of symptoms we may encounter."

I wrote "Inadequate Performance" in the first box. "If the app has functionality that matches some of the business need, but doesn't have enough of it, or is missing a couple of pieces, the BRM team bears some responsibility if the requirements are weak, but Vlad's AppDev team is the most likely source of the failure if the app doesn't perform to the requirements. Vlad has assured us that as part of their recursive development process they conducted extensive internal verification and have caught any bugs that might have impacted the first Asgard. We know that the back-out plan works well, as we have already used it."

"That's right," said Zak. "IT is expert level when it comes to successful back-outs. We have lots of practice."

Megan didn't say anything this time, but I couldn't help but think that if being good at back-outs is one of the highpoints of this company's IT team, then there was a lot of room for improvement. But I held my tongue. Since the two other people in the room were waiting for any opportunity to toss me under the bus, I didn't want to give them any additional ammunition.

"At the same time, Vlad's team owns the responsibility for training. If people cannot effectively and efficiently use the new app because of a lack of training or documentation, then his team is probably the cause of that issue. Both of them insisted that the material they prepared for Asgard would still be appropriate for users and the service desk agents supporting Asgard v2.0. But just to be on the safe side, Vlad's team was conducting some additional sessions and that meshes nicely with IT's communications campaign announcing the re-launch, and the details that may be relevant for each constituency. The most challenging part is that while you can force people to attend a training class, you cannot make them learn anything if they are not interested."

I pulled out my notes from our meetings with the rest of the stockholders.

"We also spoke with Ratana, whose QA team was working on revalidating the use cases and requirements Shallah's BRM team had provided against the revised Asgard app that Vlad's team updated from last weekend. According to her they have confirmed that the complete list of known defects has been remediated by the AppDev team and she actually took the additional step of testing the deployment in the QA environment to ensure that the roll-out itself would go smoothly."

"It sounds like you have been quite thorough … given the time you had to work with, in contacting some of the key players," said Megan. "It looks like my initial assessment of you, Chris, was correct … that you do know what you are doing."

I treated that comment as nothing but hot air. Here I had the person who hired me giving me a compliment, at the same time she'd set me up to fail.

Zak added, "Well there are more that need to be reviewed, but we tried to work with the time we had. We managed to squeeze in a meeting with Juan from sales and marketing to get the customer perspective on the release. We also talked with Madhu in finance to get his feedback on the monetary implications of our options. With the two of us we were able to cover a lot of ground."

I was putting the rest of the players into the grid on the whiteboard and said, "I'm a believer in the 'Big Tent' concept. The more players we get involved in the evaluation, the better the solution we can build. Although in this case, it seems that the functional teams are doing their jobs subject to the limitations of time and resources from this quick turnaround. But I have to say again that we really should consider taking more time and putting more resources into understanding the true root cause of the failures last week. Senior leadership is taking an enormous risk."

"It's always too little time and too few resources," said Megan. "That's the way business is today. We need to be agile and adaptive. You never have all the information you need. You make a call based on your experience and your instincts, then go with it. That's how it's done and that's how we do it in this organization."

I nodded out of politeness, but really wanted to yell at her that while it was a dynamic environment out there, it was not acceptable to treat it as an excuse to avoid systematically examining what had happened – to just deploy the app again and hope for the best, rather than thoroughly resolving the known errors and uncovering any not yet known issues.

Megan stood up, picked up her tablet and headed for the door. "I need to go give our CEO, my boss, an update and projection for success this weekend," she said. "And I'm sure you still have a lot of work to do before tomorrow night. So why don't you both go get busy"?

I started thumbing through my documents, "Would you like some notes or background material before you go"?

Megan shook her head, "No thanks, I don't need them." She pointed to her head. "Besides, the only message that is really important is that our new release manager ... Chris, has determined that the re-release of Asgard will be a success, with no impact on business operations ... that we are good to go."

My heart sank. There was no way that was going to happen and now she was officially throwing me in front of that bus speeding toward us. By dumping responsibility for the decision on me in front of her boss, protected her and Zak from any downside, but would still let them bask in any reflected glory if by some chance it actually all worked.

Megan opened the door and while standing in the doorway said, "Don't forget to be on-site in the war room on Saturday night during the maintenance window. I'm counting on the two of you to manage the deployment in person so we can keep control over the process. I'd be here, but I have another commitment. But you should be able to message me via cell phone. I know I can trust and count on you to make it happen."

With that, Megan stepped out of her office and was gone.

Zak stood up and started out the door behind her, adding his own, "Great job, Chris. I always knew you'd be a success."

Now I knew I was doomed.

Knowledge that would have helped Chris

- It is quite common for decision makers to resist wading through data used to develop recommendations or even execution details. They understand these are necessary to both implement the solution and deploy it in the production environment. They expect you to have prepared them and trust that you have done it correctly. Instead, what they want is a choice of alternatives and a recommendation. From that, they want to apply their experience and judgment to direct you how to proceed. And of course they will require follow-up and updates as to whether or not it was successful. In short, they don't want to be bothered with the details.
- To give leadership the confidence you have done your due diligence, bring the information with you, show

them that you have it, but never be disappointed that they do not want to read those details you spent hours of your life assembling. It wasn't for nothing. They want you over prepared. It makes them feel you are smart and in command of the issue so they can be comfortable relying on your recommendations.

CHAPTER 13: DEPLOY – THE END OF THE BEGINNING

I opened the door to the conference room. It was completely dark inside ... no windows ... no emergency exit signs ... nothing but a visual absence. The room had that over-lived, under-cleaned, stale panic sweat smell conference rooms all seem to exude.

I stuck my arm into the dark and fumbled along the wall until my fingers tripped over a bank of switches. I didn't bother with trying to guess the right one. I turned them all on and headed into the room.

This one was worse than usual. Not only was it the land of broken chairs, but the table was chipped on the edges with deep scratches running part way down its length. The whiteboard at the end of the room was scarred with the ghostly outlines of the wrong kinds of markers ... figures and pictures that would never be erased. I hooked up my laptop and lit up the LCD projector hanging from the ceiling. The image was almost monochromatic ... a jaundiced yellow hue was the best it could muster. I couldn't figure out if it was a bad bulb or the circuitry dying. I tried to be upbeat by reminding myself that I'd worked in worse environments and at least the ceiling wasn't leaking. Although the water stains on the tiles overhead made me hope I was not being too optimistic.

Why this room had been reserved for us was beyond me. Who else would be in the building at 11 pm on a Saturday night and need a conference room? But according to our administrator, all the other rooms were reserved and she would not double-book them, no matter how I pleaded.

I was a few minutes early, but I wanted to be there and get the conference bridge set up so we would be ready to go when everyone arrived. I put the box of coffee shop brew that I'd brought on the side table and put out the bagels, donuts and fruit I'd brought along. I always like to fire people up with lots of caffeine and sugar for meetings like this. It always seemed to keep them awake and thinking.

I opened the phone bridge and although a little disappointed that no one was waiting to join, it was still early. I wrote the timeline, activities and owners on the whiteboard, then opened up the video conference line.

After that, there wasn't much left to do but wait for the rest to arrive. The owners of each step in the release lifecycle had all accepted the meeting and I had verbally confirmed it with them. Zak and I had met with each of them during our discovery and it was important that they be part of the launch. They needed to be able to marshal whatever resources were needed to resolve any small issues that might come up.

There might be a high probability that Asgard v2.0 would fail, but I was not going to give up easily. I was going to do everything in my power to give it the best chance to succeed. Having leadership make a poor decision with a low probability of success and against every recommendation I had made, did not absolve me of responsibility for failure. If it were a success, they would get credit for their wisdom and vision. If it were a failure, leadership would not remember what I had warned them about. Instead, they would blame me for failing to advise them adequately.

I checked the clock. It was getting late. Work would have to start soon, but I was still alone and getting nervous.

Suddenly, my phone buzzed a message. I opened it up. It was a selfie of Zak sitting on the curb beside his car. It had the hood up and flashers blinking. He had that maddening smile of his. The message said that he'd broken down and was waiting for the tow truck but he didn't know how long it would take, but he knew I could handle it without him. And then he had the gall to wish me good luck tonight. Like Megan, he was working hard to keep his distance from what he knew was going to be a disaster all over again.

A text from Pat followed almost immediately thereafter and simply said, "3rd Shift Team pwmz it. wl txt or cll f w'v issuz."

I couldn't believe it. I was going to be here all alone for the implementation. Everyone was running for cover.

I was seriously considering giving up completely and just going home to get a good night's sleep before I restarted my job hunt tomorrow, but the idea of giving up made me angrier than I had been since I started. I didn't care I had to rescue this company from itself. I did not quit.

Without warning, the phone lit up that someone was on the conference bridge.

I hit the speakerphone button and said, "Hello, Chris here. Who's on the call"?

I had come too far and worked too hard to give up now. I was going to make this work no matter who showed up or what it took.

I was going to do it for the customers, the users, the leadership and the team. But most of all, I was going to do it for me.

ITG RESOURCES

IT Governance Ltd sources, creates and delivers products and services to meet the real-world, evolving IT governance needs of today's organisations, directors, managers and practitioners.

The ITG website (*www.itgovernance.co.uk*) is the international one-stop-shop for corporate and IT governance information, advice, guidance, books, tools, training and consultancy. On the website you will find the following page related to the subject matter of this book:

www.itgovernance.co.uk/itil.aspx.

Publishing Services

IT Governance Publishing (ITGP) is the world's leading IT-GRC publishing imprint that is wholly owned by IT Governance Ltd.

With books and tools covering all IT governance, risk and compliance frameworks, we are the publisher of choice for authors and distributors alike, producing unique and practical publications of the highest quality, in the latest formats available, which readers will find invaluable.

www.itgovernancepublishing.co.uk is the website dedicated to ITGP. Other titles published by ITGP that may be of interest include:

- The Daniel McLean ITSM Fiction Series

  www.itgovernance.co.uk/shop/p-1526-daniel-mclean-itsm-fiction-series.aspx

- Pragmatic Application of Service Management

  www.itgovernance.co.uk/shop/p-1510-pragmatic-application-of-service-management.aspx

- ITIL Lifecycle Essentials

  www.itgovernance.co.uk/shop/p-1285-itil-lifecycle-essentials.aspx.

We also offer a range of off-the-shelf toolkits that give comprehensive, customisable documents to help users create the specific documentation they need to properly implement a management system or standard. Written by experienced practitioners and based on the latest best practice, ITGP toolkits can save months of work for organisations working towards compliance with a given standard.

For further information please see the following page:

www.itgovernance.co.uk/shop/c-129-toolkits.aspx.

Books and tools published by IT Governance Publishing (ITGP) are available from all business booksellers and the following websites:

www.itgovernance.eu   *www.itgovernanceusa.com*

www.itgovernance.in   *www.itgovernancesa.co.za*

www.itgovernance.asia.

Training Services

If you're managing a project in your organisation, you may be interested in IT Governance's range of project management training courses, accredited by the PMI® (Project Management Institute).

The PMI's CAPM® (Certified Associate in Project Management) and PMP® (Project Management Professional) qualifications are globally recognised, and highly sought-after by professional project managers throughout the world.

CAPM

The entry-level CAPM qualification is aimed at relatively new project managers and others involved in project management who seek professional accreditation or an initial understanding of the PMBOK® Guide approach to project management.

IT Governance holds two CAPM courses:

- CAPM Certification Exam Preparation Workshop *www.itgovernance.co.uk/shop/p-419-capm-certification-exam-preparation-workshop-training-course.aspx*.
- Preparing for the CAPM Exam Training Course *www.itgovernance.co.uk/shop/p-1040-preparing-for-the-capm-exam-training-course.aspx*.

PMP

Aimed at more experienced project managers, the PMP qualification is recognised globally as an indication that holders have the experience, education and competency to lead and direct projects.

IT Governance holds two PMP courses:

- Preparing for the PMP Exam Training Course *www.itgovernance.co.uk/shop/p-1041-preparing-for-the-pmp-exam-training-course.aspx*.
- The Complete PMP Training Course *www.itgovernance.co.uk/shop/p-1164-the-complete-pmp-project-management-professional-training-course.aspx*.

For more information on all of IT Governance's PMBOK training courses, please visit *www.itgovernance.co.uk/pmbok-course.aspx*.

Professional Services and Consultancy

At IT Governance we recognise the importance of delivering services that are business-led, rather than shaped by technology. Whether you need an extra pair of hands or in-depth project support during the implementation phase, we can help you to ensure a 100% successful outcome.

If you're conducting an ITIL adoption or ISO/IEC 20000 implementation project, the IT Governance professional services team can tailor a package of consultancy, training and project resources to meet all your requirements.

With a clear focus on developing your knowledge, skills and confidence through our value-for-money approach, we will enable every member of your staff to take ownership of the improvement process and deliver consistently high-quality, efficient and effective IT services.

Our consultants will help you design IT services that will have the correct utility and warranty for your organisation and users. Having worked with many organisations during this stage of other ITSM, ITIL and ISO 20000 projects, we understand the common issues and will help you to overcome them.

For more information on out ITSM, ITIL and ISO 20000 consultancy, please visit *www.itgovernance.co.uk/itsm-itil-iso20000-consultancy.aspx*.

Newsletter

IT governance is one of the hottest topics in business today, not least because it is also the fastest moving.

You can stay up to date with the latest developments across the whole spectrum of IT governance subject matter, including; risk management, information security, ITIL and IT service management, project governance, compliance and so much more, by subscribing to ITG's core publications and topic alert emails.

Simply visit our subscription centre and select your preferences: *www.itgovernance.co.uk/newsletter.aspx*.

EU for product safety is Stephen Evans, The Mill Enterprise Hub, Stagreenan, Drogheda, Co. Louth, A92 CD3D, Ireland. (servicecentre@itgovernance.eu)